Cuba

Nicaragua

9

10

KARL MARX: THE LEGACY

DAVID McLELLAN

KARL MARX: THE LEGACY

From the BBC TV Series written and presented
by Asa Briggs

BRITISH BROADCASTING CORPORATION

Acknowledgements

I am grateful to many friends and colleagues for helping me improve the following pages. They include John Dekker, Deborah Derrick, Lesley Holmes, Victoria Huxley, John Mair, Daphne Skillen and, especially, Gay Mitchell.

Picture Credits

Black and White

BBC HULTON PICTURE LIBRARY pages 8, 29, 44, 83, 124, 157, 168, 174; BRITISH LIBRARY page 37 (lower); BRITISH MUSEUM page 82; CAMERA PRESS LTD pages 15 (lower), 110 (APN), 132 (Bernard Charlon), 135 (NCNA), 142 (Bob Wales), 146 (BTA), 148 & 150 (Prensa Latina), 171 (Isa Venturati), 177 (Leon Herschtritt); CHRIS CAPSTICK page 34; COMMUNIST PARTY PICTURE LIBRARY page 162; ILLUSTRATED LONDON NEWS page 36; IMPERIAL WAR MUSEUM page 101; INTERNATIONAL INSTITUTE OF SOCIAL HISTORY, AMSTERDAM pages 15 (right) & 40; KEYSTONE PRESS AGENCY LTD pages 103, 126 (both), 130, 140 & 155; JAMES KLUGMANN COLLECTION page 52; MANSELL COLLECTION pages 17, 50, 77, 79, 81 (top); MARX INSTITUTE, EAST BERLIN page 57; MARX MEMORIAL LIBRARY pages 25 & 37 (top); NOVOSTI PRESS AGENCY pages 70, 74, 81 (lower), 99, 106 & 113; POPPERFOTO pages 76, 91, 115 (UPI), 128, 136, 141, 152, 160 & 165; EDGAR SNOW page 121; TASS page 86; JOHN TOPHAM PICTURE LIBRARY page 117; ULLSTEIN BILDERDIENST pages 11 & 16; U.S.S.R. IN CONSTRUCTION pages 63, 65 & 92.

Colour

BRIDGEMAN ART LIBRARY (Lords Gallery, London) Anti-Trotsky Poster; CAMERA PRESS LTD Little Red Book and Castro (Christian Belpaire); J.R. FREEMAN Red Ploughman; THE JOHN HILLELSON AGENCY LTD Crêche (Bruno Barbey/Magnum), Orthodox service and May Day Parade (Elliott Erwitt/Magnum); MANSELL COLLECTION Paris Commune; POPPERFOTO Castro mural.

Published by the
British Broadcasting Corporation
35 Marylebone High Street
London W1M 4AA

ISBN 0 563 20119 3

First published 1983
© David McLellan 1983

Set in Monophoto Ehrhardt,
11pt leaded 2pts

Printed in Great Britain by
Jolly & Barber Ltd, Rugby,
Warwickshire

CONTENTS

1

THE POINT IS TO CHANGE IT

The biography of a single individual can in no way be separated from the biographies of previous and contemporary individuals: indeed, it is determined by them.

Karl Marx

A century ago Karl Marx died in his armchair in the study of his fashionable house on the northern outskirts of London. Friedrich Engels, Marx's life-long friend and supporter, used to visit him every day. On 14 March 1883 he went as usual and described the scene confronting him as follows:

> The house was in tears, it seemed that the end had come. I asked for information, tried to get a realistic view of the situation and to offer comfort. There had been a small haemorrhage and a sudden deterioration had set in. Our good old Lenchen (the maid) who cared for him as no mother ever did for her child, went up and then came down again: he was half-asleep, would I come with her? When we entered, he sat there sleeping, but never to wake any more. In two minutes he had quietly and painlessly passed away.

Marx died both intestate and stateless, which epitomised his contempt for bourgeois society and his internationalism. He did just rate a small obituary in *The Times* but the startling inaccuracies it contained showed how little he was known at the time of his death.

In a speech delivered at Marx's funeral to a handful of faithful friends, Engels declared that 'his name will live on through the centuries and so will his work'. This prediction has indeed proved correct. In the century after his death Karl Marx has attained a world fame and influence such as few men have achieved.

Marx claimed not only that he had discovered and explained the laws of motion of society, he also asserted that these laws showed that society could and would be changed by the very people without power – the working class. They were to create a new society, through a revolution. Marx argued that this revolutionary change was not only desirable: it was inevitable. To him, this was a science, like biology.

On his massive tombstone in Highgate cemetery is carved Marx's saying that 'Philosophers have only interpreted the world in various ways; the point is to change it'. While Karl Marx lived, the world did indeed change – and some of the changes were ones that he had not predicted. But capitalism was not overthrown. The revolution did not succeed anywhere in his lifetime. Yet in one generation, just thirty-four years after his death, the whole world was profoundly changed as a direct consequence of his life and work. From his grave, Marx inspired the Russian Revolution of November 1917, one of the truly cataclysmic events in world history, and the world has not been the same since.

For one third of the world, the ideas of Marx now serve to justify the established order, and to give it authority. Here, Marxism serves as the cement of society. Here, Marxism stands for the opposite of revolution. Here, Marxism means *order*, although one of which Marx himself might never have approved. Indeed, some of the things done in the name of Marxism would make Marx himself turn in his grave – if only he were not kept immobile by the immense weight of marble and bronze pressing down upon him.

Soviet leaders Krushchev and Bulganin laying a wreath at Marx's tomb in Highgate Cemetery, April 1956

8 KARL MARX: THE LEGACY

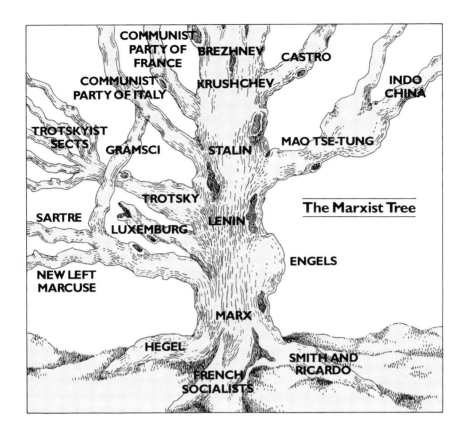

COMMUNIST
PARTY OF
FRANCE
BREZHNEV
CASTRO
COMMUNIST
PARTY OF ITALY
KRUSHCHEV
INDO
CHINA
TROTSKYIST
SECTS
GRAMSCI
STALIN
MAO TSE-TUNG
TROTSKY
The Marxist Tree
SARTRE
LUXEMBURG
LENIN
ENGELS
NEW LEFT
MARCUSE
MARX
HEGEL
SMITH AND
RICARDO
FRENCH
SOCIALISTS

Curiously enough, Marx himself gave very little indication of what a Marxist society ought to look like. All Marx's own comments on the nature of a future communist society are extremely sketchy. He had much more to say about capitalism than he did about communism. It was Marx's most celebrated disciple Lenin who was responsible for attempting to construct a Marxist society after leading Marx's Russian followers to victory in the revolution of 1917. Lenin never knew Marx. He was only a very young boy when Marx died and was brought up in a completely different setting. Lenin reshaped the legacy of Marx, and became part of an extended legacy. That 'extended legacy' is now usually called Marxism-Leninism. The success of Lenin and his fellow-revolutionaries put Marxism on the world map and meant that ever since for most people Marxism has been closely associated with Soviet Russia.

The revolution of 1917 marks the divide between the old world and the world we live in today. Already it has slipped far back into history. From the death of Marx in 1883, to the Russian revolution in 1917, is one generation. From 1917, another generation brings Russia to the death of Stalin – the man who succeeded Lenin as ruler of Russia; and since the death of Stalin, another generation of young people has grown up. The world's first Marxist state – if you like to call it that – is two-thirds of a century old and few of the citizens of this, the first socialist state, can remember any other form of society. For these people, this is socialism, this is what Karl Marx intended and this is what Lenin led them to. This is what they themselves have created – a new, socialist society. For many years after 1917 the Russians were the only nation that could claim to be governed on something like Marxist lines. It is Russian power which has meant that the Marxist-Leninist legacy has become the mainstream.

Nevertheless, there are many different kinds of Marxist approaches and many different kinds of Marxist state. Russia's neighbour China, for example, has followed a Marxist road for more than a third of a century. And China's leaders have for a long time denounced the Russian Communist leadership. They call them 'revisionists' who have 'betrayed' the revolution. Since the death of Mao Tse-tung that sort of criticism has been somewhat muted. But while Mao lived he showed perhaps the greatest originality and insight of any Communist leader of a Marxist state. He tried to put Marxism into very long-term perspective. He thought not in terms of generations, but centuries; and he tried to grapple with basic questions of human motivation, work and leisure, and how to maintain the revolutionary energy *after* the revolution has been won.

Nearer home, the People's Republic of Yugoslavia is a Marxist state, one that was created as a copy of the very first Marxist state. Yet scarcely three years after its creation, the Russian Marxist leaders denounced the Yugoslav Marxist leaders as traitors to the revolution, as enemies of Marxism. And throughout their long and sometimes bitter quarrel both the Russian leaders and the Yugoslav leaders have claimed that they alone are the true inheritors of Marx's original ideas.

It is not only in Marxist states that Marx's ideas have had influence. Throughout the rest of the world, he has changed the way people *think*. Whether we agree with him or not, Marx has shaped our ideas about society. He built up a system which draws on philosophy, on history, on economics and on politics. And although the professional philosophers, the economists and the political scientists often do not accept his theories, they cannot ignore them. They have become part of the mental scaffolding of the century with the result that a lot of our thinking about history and society is a dialogue with Marx's ghost.

To understand what Marx himself meant, a lot of history has to be stripped away. For Marx's ideas have been overlaid by many different interpretations and have been used to justify many different sorts of politics. To

The house in which Marx was born in Trier, Germany on 5 May 1818. The Marx family occupied two rooms on the ground floor and three on the first floor

understand Marx before Marxism we have to go back to Trier, a quiet market town on the River Moselle in Germany where he was born on 5 May 1818. Trier imbued Marx with his abiding passion for history. For Trier had not always been a backwater. It was the oldest city in Germany. Under the name of Augusta Trevirorum the city had been considered the Rome of the North and served as the headquarters of the most powerful of the Roman armies. The Porta Nigra, in whose shadow (literally) Marx grew up, and the enormous fourth-century basilica were enduring monuments of Trier's past imperial glory. In the Middle Ages the city had been the seat of a Prince-Archbishop whose lands stretched as far as Metz, Toul and Verdun; it was said that it contained more churches than any other German city of comparable size. More recently, Trier had had its share of the grim realities of underdevelopment then characteristic of Germany. The town had very little industry and its inhabitants were mainly officials, traders and artisans who activities were bound up with the famous Moselle vineyards whose prosperity was on the decline. The consequent unemployment and high prices caused increases in beggary, prostitution and emigration; more than a quarter of the city's population subsisted entirely on public charity.

Like many of his followers, Marx was born into a comfortable middle-class home. At the time of his birth, his father, Heinrich Marx, was counsellor-at-law to the High Court of Appeal in Trier; he also practised in the Trier County Court, and was awarded the title of *Justizrat* (very roughly the equivalent of a British QC). For many years he was president of the city lawyers' association and occupied a respected position in Trier society.

In order to preserve his post, Heinrich Marx had to renounce Judaism and convert to Protestantism. It would be difficult to find anyone who had a more Jewish ancestry than Karl Marx: almost all the rabbis of Trier from the sixteenth century onwards were included among his ancestors on his father's side and his mother, who was Dutch, was no less steeped in rabbinical tradition than her husband. Some have considered this rabbinic ancestry to be the key to Marx's ideas and seen him as a secularised version of an Old Testament prophet. This must of necessity be highly speculative but what is certain is that his Jewishness made Marx an outsider who could never be completely integrated into existing society. The experience of prejudice and discrimination are powerful arguments for changing society and most of Marx's principal followers in Germany and Russia were also of Jewish origin.

Nevertheless, Marx's father wore his Jewishness very lightly. What chiefly inspired him were the views of the eighteenth-century French rationalists and he shared their limitless faith in the power of reason to explain and improve the world. The Rhineland had been annexed by France for the

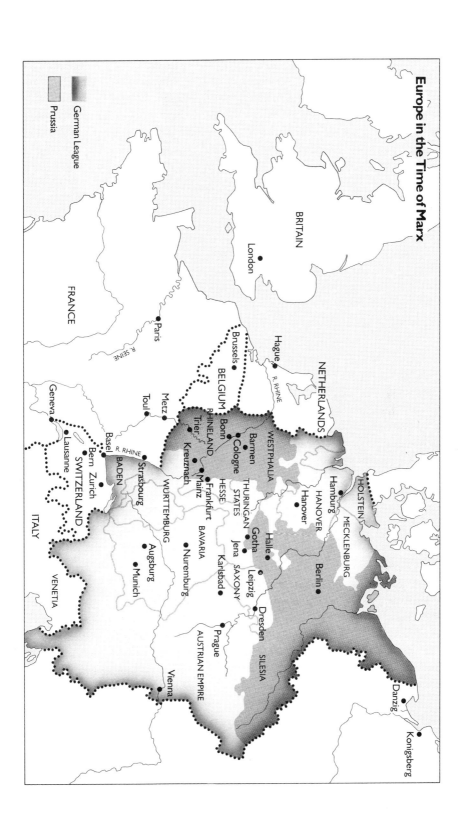

Europe in the Time of Marx

Prussia

German League

BRITAIN

London

FRANCE

Paris

R. SEINE

Geneva

Lausanne

SWITZERLAND

Bern   Zurich

Basel

R. RHINE

ITALY

VENETIA

Toul

Metz

Strasbourg

BADEN

WURTTEMBURG

Augsburg

Munich

Brussels

BELGIUM

Hague

R. RHINE

NETHERLANDS

Bonn

RHINELAND

Trier   Cologne   Barmen

Kreuznach

Mainz

Frankfurt

HESSE

THURINGAN STATES

BAVARIA

Nuremburg

Karlsbad

Prague

AUSTRIAN EMPIRE

Vienna

WESTPHALIA

Gotha

Jena

SAXONY

Leipzig

Halle

Dresden

SILESIA

HANOVER

Hamburg

Hanover

HOLSTEIN

MECKLENBURG

Berlin

Danzig

Konigsberg

twenty years following the French Revolution of 1789 and the new French ideas had gained much influence there. According to this view, men were by nature all good and equally rational; the cause of human misery was simply ignorance, which resulted partly from unsatisfactory material circumstances and partly from a deliberate distortion or suppression of the truth by those in authority, whether civil or religious, in whose obvious interest it was to perpetuate the deceptions under which mankind laboured. One of the chief means of altering this state of affairs was education; another was change in material conditions.

How much these ideas affected the young Marx we do not know but they were certainly prevalent at the Trier High School which he attended from 1830 to 1835. Intellectually, Marx was above average, though not outstanding, being equal eighth in a class of thirty-two. He is also said to have been 'both loved and feared by his fellow pupils, loved because he was always ready for boyish pranks and feared for the ease with which he composed satirical verses and lampoons against his enemies'. This gift for biting satire stayed with him all his life.

Apart from home and school, there was a third important influence on the young Marx – the von Westphalen family. The von Westphalens were a recently ennobled family who lived in a fine house quite near the Marxes. The Baron von Westphalen, whose mother had been descended from the Earls of Argyll, was a man of liberal and progressive views and devoted a lot of time to the young Marx. They went for intellectual walks together and the Baron read him Homer and Shakespeare who remained favourite authors all his life. He also interested Marx in the idea of Utopian socialism put forward by such French writers as Fourier and Saint Simon. Socialist ideas were a reaction to the dislocation and growing disparity of wealth caused by the early industrial revolution: they proposed schemes for the thorough reorganisation of society whereby goods and services would be distributed according to people's needs; and they were dubbed Utopian in that they offered no indication of how these schemes might come to be put into practice.

But socialism was not Marx's central concern when in October 1835 he left home to sail down the Moselle and Rhine to the University of Bonn. Although ostensibly there to study law, he did not stay long. When not drinking and duelling, Marx passed most of his time writing poetry and spending more money than his family could afford – another lifelong characteristic. Well before the end of the academic year, Heinrich Marx decided that one year at Bonn was quite enough and that his son should transfer to the University of Berlin. But another problem soon arose. 'Scarcely was the wild rampaging in Bonn finished', wrote his father, 'scarcely were

Left: Marx in 1836, aged 18. The picture is taken from a lithograph of a student group at the University of Bonn. *Right:* The young Jenny von Westphalen, Marx's future wife, in 1835

your debts paid – and they were really of the most varied nature – when to our dismay the sorrows of love appeared.' Jenny von Westphalen was four years older that the young Marx and they had been friends from their earliest childhood. With her dark auburn hair and green eyes Jenny was widely noticed in Trier and had even been chosen as Queen of the Ball. The young Marx, who later described himself as 'a really furious Roland' was an insistent suitor; there had been an understanding between them before Marx left for Bonn and in the summer of 1836 this was turned into a formal engagement.

Marx was to spend almost five years in Berlin, a city in almost total contrast to Bonn. Engels later graphically recalled the Berlin of the time 'with its scarcely formed bourgeoisie, its loud-mouthed petty bourgeoisie, so unenterprising and fawning, its still completely unorganised workers, its masses of bureaucrats and hangers-on of nobility and court, its whole character as mere "residence".' The dominant philosophy in Berlin was that of Hegel, and Marx quickly fell under its spell. It was probably the most important intellectual step of Marx's whole life. He wrote to his father: 'A curtain had fallen, my holy of holies was rent asunder and new gods had to be installed. I left behind idealism . . . and came to seek the idea in the real itself. If the Gods had before dwelt above the earth, they had now become its centre.'

The Humboldt University in Berlin in the time of Marx who spent five years here as a rather maverick student

Hegel was the first philosopher to put *change* at the centre of his thought. Previous philosophers had tended to deal in static, unchanging concepts: for Hegel there were no eternal verities, only the history of the human spirit constantly transcending itself in the search for an ever more complete understanding of things. The motor of this change was *conflict*: conflict lay at the heart of everything, for every culture, system of thought contained within itself the seeds of its own destruction. The history of Spirit or Mind was like a huge thrusting tree constantly bursting through its old bark to produce new shoots which themselves, in turn, give way to fresher and larger growth. This was what Hegel meant by dialectic: the process of incessant conflict pushing history to new heights. Now Marx was enormously impressed by the encyclopaedic character of Hegel's system and its optimistic dynamic of inevitable progress through conflict – indeed he speaks of being 'seduced' by Hegel. But what he *didn't* like in Hegel was the preoccupation with ideas: for Marx it made more sense to start with the material reality of human beings, their basic need for food, clothing, shelter and the way they satisfied these needs through the tools at their disposal, the property relationships they created and the consequent classes into which society was split. It was here – in the conflicts of the material and social world – that the dialectic was to be found. This is what Marx meant by saying that he found Hegel standing on his head and stood him on his feet.

The German philosopher Hegel lecturing in Berlin in 1828. Hegel's dialectical vision of the world remained a major influence on Marx's thought

On his conversion to Hegelianism, Marx joined the Doctors' Club, a gathering of rather bohemian intellectuals who formed the focal point of the Young Hegelians as the radical disciples of Hegel were called. Its central figure was Bruno Bauer an atheist who lectured in theology at the University of Berlin. One of the members of the Club has left us this vivid description of Marx in a satirical poem on Club members:

> But who advances here full of impetuosity?
> It is a dark form from Trier, an unleashed monster,
> With self-assured step he hammers the ground with his heels
> And raises his arms in full fury to heaven
> As though he wished to seize the celestial vault and lower it to
>   earth.
> In rage he continually deals with his redoubtable fist,
> As if a thousand devils were gripping his hair.

His father was not so appreciative: 'Alas, your conduct has consisted merely in disorder, meandering in all the fields of knowledge, musty traditions by sombre lamplight; degeneration in a learned dressing gown with uncombed hair has replaced degeneration with a beer glass'. The final report on Marx's university career declared that he had several times been sued for debt and changed his address at least ten times during his five-year stay. He did, however, manage to finish his doctoral thesis. The subject was the rather obscure one of ancient Greek atomic philosophy where Marx was concerned to contrast the views of Epicurus, who introduced the idea of spontaneity into the movement of the atoms, with those of Democritus for whom atoms moved in a strictly determined order. Marx was awarded his doctorate in 1841. His student days were over and it was time to look for a job.

There are few things more dangerous than an unemployed intellectual. If the young Karl Marx had now got what he really wanted, things might have gone very differently for the world. He wanted an academic post in a university. But the government was becoming more reactionary. His friend Bauer was, not surprisingly, dismissed and the outlook was bleak. So instead Marx went back to his own part of Germany and did the next best thing: he became a journalist and learned how to communicate his ideas. And in the course of his journalism he also became an active revolutionary. Marx's journalistic articles are masterpieces of polemical exegesis, demonstrating the great pamphleteering talent that he was to exhibit throughout his life. All his early articles – and, to a lesser extent, many of his later writings – were written in an extremely vivid style: his radical and uncompromising approach, his love of polarisation, his method of dealing with opponents' views by *reductio ad absurdum*, all led him to write in stark opposites. Marx moved to Cologne, the capital of the Rhineland, in April 1842 and six months later was offered the editorship of the leading liberal paper there – the *Rheinische Zeitung*. One of the newspaper's leading backers wrote of Marx at the time:

> Karl Marx from Trier was a powerful man of twenty-four whose thick black hair sprung from his cheeks, arms, nose and ears. He was domineering, impetuous, passionate, full of boundless self-confidence, but at the same time deeply earnest and learned, an indefatigable dialectician who with his restless Jewish penetration pushed every proposition of Young Hegelian doctrine to its final conclusion and was already then, by his concentrated study of economics, preparing his conversion to communism. Under Marx's leadership the young newspaper soon began to speak very recklessly . . .

The *Rheinische Zeitung* flourished in an atmosphere quite different from that of Berlin: Rhineland-Westphalia, annexed by France from 1795 to 1814, had had the benefit of economic, political and administrative reforms. Textile production made the Ruhr one of the most industrialised regions of Europe and the *Rheinische Zeitung* was financed by these industrialists to promote their liberal social and economic doctrines. The climate of opinion in Cologne was particularly favourable to the reception of socialist ideas: the Rhineland liberals (unlike their Manchester counterparts) were very socially conscious and considered that the State had far-reaching duties towards society. Socialist ideas did not originate or initially take root among the German working classes. Germany was only just beginning to become an industrialised country and industrial workers were only a minute proportion of the population. The industrial workers did not have sufficient organisation and, being mostly ex-artisans, were nostalgic for the past rather than revolutionary. Socialism was first spread by a part of the intellectual élite, who saw the proletarian masses as an instrument of social renewal. Socialist ideas were propagated by such writers as Moses Hess, the first German communist, who had picked up his communism in Paris after running away from his father's factory in Cologne. In a mystical and meandering fashion he proclaimed the idea of the polarisation of classes and the imminence of a proletarian revolution. It was Hess who converted to communism the rebellious son of one of the Ruhr's leading capitalists – Friedrich Engels. Another prominent figure of the time was the itinerant tailors' leader Wilhelm Weitling who, in messianic tones, defended, against the rich and powerful of the earth who caused all inequality and injustice, the right of all to education and happiness by means of social equality and justice.

Marx had little sympathy for the moralistic socialism of Hess and Weitling. His own path to socialism originated in his investigative journalism. Engels said later that he had 'always heard from Marx that it was precisely through concentrating on the law of thefts of wood and the situation of the Moselle winegrowers, that he was led from pure politics to economic relationships and so to socialism'. In his first important article as editor of the *Rheinische Zeitung* Marx discussed the more stringent laws recently proposed in regard to thefts of timber. The gathering of dead wood had traditionally been unrestricted, but the scarcities caused by the agrarian crises of the 1820s and the growing needs of industry had led to legal controls. The situation had become unmanageable: more than five-sixths of all prosecutions in the Rhineland dealt with wood. Marx attacked the proposed changes in the law which would mean that dead things would maintain a secret domination over living men; the natural relation of domination and possession was reversed, and human beings were determined by timber which had now become a commodity. Marx's subsequent exposure of the poverty widespread among the Moselle winegrowers was just as biting and finally caused the suppression of the newspaper. Marx was not dismayed. 'The government,' he said, 'has given me back my liberty.' His decision to leave Germany was already taken: the only questions were when and where to go.

But before emigration Marx had an important matter to attend to. He had now been engaged for more than seven years and it was high time he got married. As soon as the *Rheinische Zeitung* had been suppressed, Marx went to the spa of Kreuznach, about fifty miles east of Trier, where Jenny and her mother had temporarily moved probably to avoid difficulties with Jenny's stepbrother Ferdinand, a career civil servant and later Prussian Minister of the Interior. The wedding took place in the Protestant Church and registry office in Kreuznach on 19 June 1843. The official registration describes the couple as 'Herr Karl Marx, Doctor of Philosophy, residing in Cologne and Fraulein Johanna Bertha Julie Jenny von Westphalen, no occupation, residing in Kreuznach'. Marx and Jenny left immediately for a honeymoon of several weeks. They first went to Switzerland to see the Rhine Falls near Schaffhausen and then – travelling through the province of Baden – they took their time on the journey back to Kreuznach. Jenny later told a story that illustrated how extraordinarily irresponsible they both were (and continued to be) in their attitude to money. Jenny's mother had given them some money for the honeymoon and they took it with them, in a chest. They had it beside them in the coach during their journey and took it into the different hotels. When they had visits from needy friends they left it open on the table in their room and anyone could take as much as he pleased. Needless to say, it was soon empty.

Given this growing interest in socialist revolution, it was natural that Marx should decide to emigrate to France. At that time France was *the* revolutionary country and the French Revolution of 1789 was still *the* revolution which inspired revolutionaries then in much the same way as the Bolshevik revolution of 1917 does many present-day Marxists. It was his reading of the history of the French revolution in the summer of 1843 that showed Marx the role of class struggle in social development. There had been another revolution in 1830 and a third revolution was widely expected in the 1840s. If France was the revolutionary country, then Paris was the revolutionary capital and every would-be revolutionary looked to Paris for inspiration. As Marx put it, 'the day of German resurrection will be heralded by the crowing of the Gallic cock'.

In order to further this Franco-German co-operation, Marx intended to publish in Paris a journal which combined articles both by the radical German Hegelians and by the French socialists. His collaborator in this project was Arnold Ruge a fellow Young Hegelian of independent means and also an exile from German universities on account of his progressive views. But contact with the French proved difficult. There was a bewildering variety of every conceivable kind of sect, salon and newspaper each proclaiming some form of socialism. The French were put off by the Germans' advocacy of atheism and materialism, watchwords of pre-1789 thought that they now considered out-of-date. In the event, the journal appeared without a single French contribution.

Nevertheless, in the articles he wrote himself, Marx was breaking new ground. He came to see that the principles of 1789 – political liberty and equality – were not enough. For they had not solved the basic problem of the social redistribution of wealth. The Rights of Man so fervently proclaimed by the revolutionaries of 1789 and the framers of the United States constitution did not in fact make all citizens free and equal. For without the economic wherewithal to make use of these rights they remained abstract and hollow. It was all very well to say that the Grill Room of the Ritz was open to everyone, that all were free and equal in their right to enter: the fact remained that only a very restricted section of the population were to be found there enjoying their splendid dinners – those who had the money to pay the bill. Liberty and equality, therefore, should not be considered primarily from a political point of view but from a social and economic one. Purely political liberty, for example, 'the right to do and perform what does not harm others', was, according to Marx, 'not based on the union of man with man but on the separation of man from man. It is the right to this separation, the right of the limited individual who is limited to himself'. Property, the right to dispose of one's possessions as one wills without regard to others, was 'the right of selfishness . . . it leads man to see in other men not the realisation, but the limitation of his own freedom'. Equality was no more than the equal right to the liberty described above, and security of property was the guarantee of egoism. The political emancipation achieved in the United States and, to some extent, in France had indeed brought about the dissolution of the old feudal order. But the change from feudal to bourgeois society had not brought *human* emancipation.

But how was this human emancipation, with its social and economic dimensions, to be achieved? It was the answer to this question that Marx found in Paris. Instead of editing a paper for the Rhineland bourgeoisie or sitting in his study in Kreuznach, he was now at the heart of socialist thought and action. The city had a large population of German immigrant workers – almost 100,000 – some had come to perfect the techniques of their various trades; some had come simply because they could find no work in Germany. Marx was immediately impressed:

When communist artisans form associations, education and propaganda are their first aims. But the very act of associating creates a new need – the need for society – and what appeared to be a means has become an end. The most striking results of this practical development are to be seen when French socialist workers meet together. Smoking, eating and drinking are no longer simply means of bringing people together. Company, association, entertainment which also has society as its aim, are sufficient for them; the brotherhood of man is no empty phrase but a reality, and the nobility of man shines forth upon us from their toil-worn bodies.

It was the destiny of the proletariat to solve the problems that had been inadequately dealt with in 1789. In messianic tones Marx proclaimed the proletariat to be

> a sphere that cannot emancipate itself without emancipating itself from all other spheres of society and thereby emancipating these other spheres themselves. In a word it is the complete loss of humanity and thus can only recover itself by a complete redemption of humanity. This dissolution of society, as a particular class, is the proletariat.

The radical tone of the journal led to a swift reaction from the German authorities. Warrants were issued for the arrest of Marx and Ruge: for the first time in his life Marx had become a political refugee. It also led to a break between Marx and Ruge who could not stand communists. 'They wish to liberate people', he wrote to his mother with the bitterness of one whose financial resources had been called upon just once too often, 'by turning them into artisans and abolishing private property by a fair and communal repartition of goods; but for the moment they attach the utmost importance to property and in particular to money'. Ruge was also rather a puritan and disapproved of Marx's bohemian life-style.

But Marx thrived on the perfervid intellectual atmosphere of Paris. Ruge might disapprove of what he considered Marx's disorderly life, cynicism and arrogance, but he had to admire his energy:

> He reads a lot. He works in an extraordinarily intense way. He has a critical talent that degenerates sometimes into something which is simply a dialectical game, but he never finishes anything – he interrupts every bit of research to plunge into a fresh ocean of books . . . He is more excited and violent than ever, especially when his work has made him ill and he has not been to bed for three or even four nights on end.

Marx spent a lot of time with the poet Heine and with his future opponent, the anarchist Bakunin. He also much enjoyed the company of Russian emigré aristocrats who fêted him throughout his stay.

During July and August 1844, however, Marx had a period of peace and quiet that he put to good use. On 1 May their first child was born – a girl, called Jenny after her mother. The baby was very sickly and Jenny took her away to Trier for two months to show her to the family there and obtain the advice of her old doctor. While his wife and baby were away, Marx made voluminous notes on classical economics, communism and Hegel. Known variously as the *Economic and Philosophical Manuscripts* or *1844 Manuscripts* or *Paris Manuscripts*, these manuscripts (when first published in 1932) were hailed by some as Marx's most important single piece of work. The manuscripts were all exploratory, disjointed, exuberant outpourings of ideas to be taken up and developed in subsequent economic writings. Here for the first time there appeared together, if not yet united, what Engels described as the three constituent elements in Marx's thought – German idealist philosophy, French socialism and English economics.

Marx's basic thesis was that the way in which human beings related together in capitalist society denied their true human nature, for they were naturally communal and co-operative. The economic organisation of capitalism, based as it was on private property, thwarted these tendencies. 'The only wheels', Marx wrote, 'that political economy sets in motion are greed and war among the greedy: competition.' The result was the general impoverishment and dehumanising of the worker that Marx called alienation. For human beings, instead of controlling and exploiting in common the product of their labour, found the reverse to be the case: the products of their labour controlled *them* in that they were subject to the unpredictable movements of the market and entrammelled by the cash nexus.

The solution that Marx proposed to this sorry state of affairs was communism. In a visionary passage, he declared:

Communism is the positive abolition of private property and thus of human self-alienation and therefore the real reappropriation of the human essence by and for man. This is communism as the complete and conscious return of man – conserving all the riches of previous development for man himself as a social, i.e. human, being. Communism as completed naturalism is humanism and as completed humanism is naturalism. It is the genuine resolution of the antagonism between man and nature and between man and man. It is the solution to the riddle of history and knows itself to be this solution.

Marx's picture of the communist individual developing many talents and freely producing in co-operation with his fellow human beings has proved attractive to all those interested in Marxism with a human face as opposed to the often dogmatic and authoritarian attitudes of later Marxist regimes. Marx's communism here also echoes abiding themes in all criticisms of industrial society – the dream of a harmony to overcome the stunting effects of the division of labour and the anti-social pursuit of private interest.

Scarcely had Marx completed these manuscripts when he met Friedrich Engels and formed a friendship that lasted until his death. Engels had been converted to radical Hegelianism and then socialism while doing his military service in Berlin. He had been sent to England to help manage the Manchester branch of the family cotton business, Ermen and Engels. While he was working in the interests of that capitalist class to which he so obviously belonged, Engels looked about him with the eyes of a revolutionary and noted the wretched state of so many of the industrial workers and their families in the manufacturing districts of Lancashire and the West Riding of Yorkshire.

Engels put his observations into a book that is still a bestseller. He called it simply *The Condition of the Working Class in England*. In it, Engels was concerned to describe the sufferings of the proletariat of England. But, like Marx, he went further. He predicted with great confidence an imminent and very bloody revolution. While in Manchester, Engels sent to Marx's journal an article entitled *Outlines of a Critique of Political Economy* whose stark and clear prediction of the impending doom of capitalism made a strong impression on Marx.

Engels passed through Paris at the end of August 1844 on his way back to Germany. He spent ten days with Marx. 'Our complete agreement in all theoretical fields became obvious', wrote Engels, 'and our joint work dates from that time.' At the end of his life, looking back on this co-operation, Engels summed up his views as follows:

> What Marx accomplished, I would not have achieved. Marx stood higher, saw further, and took a wider and quicker view than all the rest of us. Marx was a genius; we others were at best talented. Without him the theory would not, by a long way, be what it is today. It therefore rightly bears his name.

Although this probably represents an accurate account of their later relationship, in the late summer of 1844 Engels, with his practical experience of capitalism, brought more to Marx than he received.

In their similar origins in comfortable middle-class homes, their youthful enthusiasm for poetry and their transition through Young Hegelian liberalism to radical politics, Marx and Engels shared sufficient experiences to form a basis for lasting friendship. But it was a friendship more of contrasts than similarities. Marx's forte lay in his power of abstraction. He had thoroughly absorbed the Hegelian method and his dialectical approach managed to blend elements in a subtle synthesis. While Marx had been studying Hegel, Engels had been gaining practical experience and making

The young Friedrich Engels in 1845. From their meeting a year earlier, Engels was a constant friend and support to the Marx family

first-hand observations as a professional business man; always quick at getting his thoughts together, he could write fast and clearly, and sometimes with a dogmatism foreign even to Marx. Their lifestyles, too, were very different. Engels was invariably immaculately dressed, his study was always tidy, and he was precise, businesslike and responsible in money matters. Marx was careless about his clothing, had a very disorderly order in his study and had no notion of how to manage money. Marx was, moreover, very definitely a family man, however much he might sometimes regret it; Engels was a great womaniser and, although capable of long attachments, always refused marriage.

But before their collaboration could bear fruit, Marx found himself compelled to leave France. Under pressure from the Prussian government, the French Minister of the Interior issued an order expelling Marx, Heine and Ruge. Marx himself was given twenty-four hours' grace and left for Brussels. Jenny followed a few days later.

Belgium was something of a political haven for refugees as it enjoyed greater freedom of expression than any other country on the continent of Europe. It was a very rapidly industrialising country independent only since 1830 and Brussels was to be Marx's home for the next three years, a time which was probably the happiest ever enjoyed by the Marx family. Jenny found herself pregnant on arrival in Brussels and her mother now sent her own maid, Helene Demuth, a practical young baker's daughter from a village near Trier, then aged twenty-five, who had grown up in the Westphalen family from the age of eleven or twelve. She was to be the constant, if often unmentioned, companion to the family until Marx's death. There was no shortage of money: Marx had received a substantial advance for a book and Engels had organised a collection for him in the Rhineland on his expulsion from Paris. Engels and Hess soon moved in next door to the Marxes and they all formed a very jolly community.

This happy social life was the background to intense intellectual activity on Marx's part. In particular he composed (with Engels) a large book entitled *The German Ideology* which remained one of his central works. It was a tremendous achievement in view of the low level of socialist writing and thought prevalent at the time. Marx never subsequently stated his materialist conception of history at such length and in such detail. It is still a masterpiece today for the cogency and clarity of its presentation. Yet it remained unknown for almost a century, as Marx and Engels could not find a publisher. Thus, as Marx wrote later, 'we abandoned the manuscript to the gnawing of the mice all the more willingly as we had achieved our main purpose – self-clarification'. And, in fact, the manuscript as it survives does bear considerable traces of mice's teeth.

In *The German Ideology* Marx and Engels elaborated their central idea that the key to an understanding of man and his history was to look at man's productive activity. The fundamental activity of man was the way in which he obtained his means of subsistence by interaction with nature – in short, his labour. This labour was the primary factor in history and the ideas and concepts – political, philosophical or religious – through which men interpreted this activity were secondary. History was not the result of accident, nor was it shaped by the acts of great men (still less by supernatural powers): history was the – mostly unconscious – creation of labouring men, and it was subject to observable laws. In their own words:

> The way in which man produces his food depends first of all on the nature of the means of subsistence that he finds and has to reproduce. This mode of production must not be viewed simply as reproduction of the physical existence of individuals. Rather it is a definite form of their activity, a definite way of expressing their life, a definite mode of life. As individuals express their life, so they are. What they are, therefore, coincides with what they produce, and how they produce. The nature of individuals thus depends on the material conditions which determine their production.

They went on to state that 'how far the productive forces of a nation are developed is shown most evidently by the degree to which the division of labour has been developed.' They showed how the division of labour led to the separation of town and country and then to the separation of industrial from commercial labour and so on. Marx and Engels summarised their conclusions so far as follows:

> The fact is, then, that definite individuals who are productively active in a specific way enter into these definite social and political relations. The social structure and the state continually evolve out of the life-process of definite individuals, but individuals not as they may appear in their own or other people's imagination but rather as they really are, that is, as they work, produce materially, and act under definite material limitations, presuppositions, and conditions independent of their will.

They then reiterated their general approach, stating that 'consciousness does not determine life, but life determines consciousness', and showed how the division of labour, leading to private property, created social inequality, class struggle and the erection of political structures.

Marx and Engels then proclaimed the imminence of a communist revolution. The strains and stresses of capitalist society had grown to a point where the mere survival of most people made it necessary to take the means of production into common ownership. The transition to communism was inevitable: 'Communism is not for us a state of affairs still to be established, not an ideal to which reality will have to adjust. We call communism the real movement which abolishes the present state of affairs.' Thus history, for Marx and Engels, was the optimistic story of the unfolding of human potentialities culminating in communism.

Having clarified their fundamental ideas in *The German Ideology*, Marx and Engels turned their attention to impressing their new insights on the very varied existing left-wing groups. Brussels was an ideal vantage point from which to build up contacts among German socialists, for it was in the middle of a triangle formed by Paris and London (where the largest colonies of expatriate German workers had congregated) and Cologne (capital of the Rhineland, the German province by far the most receptive to communist ideas). Marx began by establishing a Communist Correspondence Committee which was to be the embryo of all future Communist Internationals. It was at a meeting of this Committee in Marx's house that there occurred the first of innumerable splits in the Communist movement. Wilhelm Weitling, famous for his emotional agitation among itinerant tailors, had been invited to the meeting. Marx attacked him for not basing his propaganda on any serious analysis of society. Weitling retorted by declaring that his modest spadework was perhaps of greater importance for the common cause than criticism and armchair analysis of doctrines far from the world of the suffering and afflicted people. 'On hearing these last words' an observer at the meeting reports,

> Marx finally lost control of himself and thumped so hard with his fist on the table that the lamp on it rung and shook. He jumped up saying: 'Ignorance never yet helped anybody!' We followed his example and left the table. The sitting ended and as Marx paced up and down the room, extraordinarily irritated and angry, I hurriedly took leave of him and his interlocutors and went home, amazed at all I had seen and heard.

Marx's opportunity to enter working class politics came in 1847 when he was invited to become a theoretical adviser to the League of the Just. The League was a semi-clandestine organisation of German emigré workers which had recently moved its headquarters from Paris to London. Under Marx's influence its name was changed from League of the Just to Communist League and its slogan 'All men are brothers' altered to 'Proletarians of all Countries – Unite'. (Marx declared that there were many men whose brother he wished on no account to be.) At the end of the year the Central Committee of the League entrusted Marx and Engels with the task of

The only surviving page, in Marx's illegible handwriting, from a draft of *The Communist Manifesto*, the founding document of Communism. The top two lines were written by Jenny Marx

drawing up a Manifesto which was to become the founding document of communism.

The *Communist Manifesto* opens with a paean of praise to the achievements of capitalism in opening up new frontiers and creating new wealth. But in praising the triumph of the capitalists, Marx and Engels also announced the doom of capitalism. Revolution was not merely something to be fought for, it was also unavoidable:

> The advance of industry, whose involuntary promoter is the bourgeoisie, replaces the isolation of the labourers, due to competition, by their revolutionary combination, due to association. The development of Modern Industry, therefore, cuts from under its feet the very foundation on which the bourgeoisie produces and appropriates products. What the bourgeoisie, therefore, produces, above all, is its own grave-diggers. Its fall and the victory of the proletariat are equally inevitable.

Among the immediate proposals of the *Manifesto* were the abolition of landed property and inheritance, the imposition of income tax, the centralisation of credit and communications, state ownership of factories, and free education. But Marx went further. In presenting a vivid history of the past as a series of class struggles, he proclaimed a new vision of the future:

> When, in the course of development, class distinctions have disappeared and all production has been concentrated in the hands of a vast association of the whole nation, the public power will lose its political character. Political power, properly so called, is merely the organised power of one class for oppressing another. If the proletariat during its contest with the bourgeoisie is compelled, by the force of circumstances, to organise itself as a class, if, by means of a revolution, it makes itself the ruling class, and as such, sweeps away by force the old conditions of production, then it will, along with these conditions, have swept away the conditions for the existence of class antagonisms and of classes generally, and will thereby have abolished its own supremacy as a class.
>
> In place of the old bourgeois society, with its classes and class antagonisms, we shall have an association, in which the free development of each is the condition for the free development of all.

Although virtually all the ideas contained in the *Communist Manifesto* had been enunciated before – particularly among the French socialists in whose tradition the *Manifesto* is firmly situated – the power and clarity of its style and the all-embracing sweep of its vision of history have made it into a classic. Of all the early socialist tracts and manifestoes which survive to this day, the one that has always been most widely used – the only one still widely read – is the *Communist Manifesto*. For millions of people it is their introduction to Marxism and Communism

Nevertheless, the publication of the *Manifesto* went virtually unnoticed. Before it was off the presses, a wave of revolutions swept across Europe. In Brussels Marx was arrested prior to being deported. Luckily for him, King

Louis Philippe in France had just been deposed and the provisional republican government invited him back to Paris. When the revolutionary tide reached Germany and even the Prussian monarchy looked unsteady, Marx decided to return to his old haunts in Cologne and became editor of a new paper called the *Neue Rheinische Zeitung* in memory of the one suppressed five years earlier. The new paper did not preach a socialist republic nor exclusively a workers' one. Its programme was universal suffrage, direct elections, the abolition of all feudal dues and charges, the establishment of a state banking system, and the admission of state responsibility for unemployment. The reason for this moderation was that the German 'revolution' had been a very partial one: only in Berlin and Vienna had there been any serious violence, and in the whole of Germany only one prince lost his throne – let alone his head. In 1848 it was only possible to modify autocratic structures: these did not entirely disappear until after the First World War. For the autocratic government managed to retain control both of the army and of the administration which was more powerful than that in either France or England. An all-German assembly was granted but proved to be little more than a talking-shop.

With the ebbing of the revolution, the authorities began to counter-attack. Marx was prosecuted on a charge of plotting to overthrow the régime. His speech in his own defence was an object lesson in the Marxist view of history:

> Society is not based on the law (he stated), that is a legal fiction, rather law must be based on society; it must be the expression of society's common interests and needs, as they arise from the various material methods of production, against the arbitrariness of the single individual. The *Code Napoléon*, which I have in my hand, did not produce modern bourgeois society. Bourgeois society, as it arose in the eighteenth century and developed in the nineteenth, merely finds its legal expression in the Code. As soon as it no longer corresponds to social relationships, it is worth no more than the paper it is written on. You cannot make old laws the foundation of a new social development any more than these old laws created the old social conditions . . . Any attempted assertion of the eternal validity of laws continually clashes with present needs, it prevents commerce and industry, and paves the way for social crises that break out with political revolutions.

Marx was acquitted and the foreman of the jury thanked him for his instructive explanation. But his days in Germany were numbered. In May 1849, the order for his expulsion was issued and the last number of the *Neue Rheinische Zeitung* appeared, printed in red. Twenty thousand copies of the

'Red Number' were sold and were soon changing hands at ten times the original price. It was even rumoured that some copies had been expensively framed, to serve as ikons.

Marx returned to Paris, still optimistic. He wrote to Engels: 'A colossal eruption of the revolutionary crater was never more imminent than now in Paris . . . I am in touch with the whole of the revolutionary party and in a few days will have *all* revolutionary journals at my disposition.' In fact, the political atmosphere was becoming more reactionary and the military autocracy of Louis Napoleon was imminent. In mid-July, as Jenny wrote: 'the familiar police sergeant came again and informed us that "Karl Marx and his wife had to leave Paris within 24 hours".' The only country left for Marx was the relatively liberal England, the final resting-place of so many political refugees of the time and the heartland of industrial capitalism from which Marx learnt so much. At the end of August 1849 Marx sailed for London in his final emigration.

2

THE ENGLISH CONNECTION

Here Marx found what he was looking for, what he needed: the bricks and mortar for his work. *Capital* could have only been written in London. Marx could only become what he did become in England.

Wilhelm Liebknecht

Marx spent more than half his life in Britain. When he arrived in late 1849 as a political refugee, he regarded his stay as merely temporary. But nothing, it is said, endures like the temporary, and so it proved with Marx: what he called his 'sleepless night of exile' lasted until his death thirty-four years later. So there is a blue plaque to commemorate Marx's first long-term residence in Dean Street, Soho (though the dates are inaccurate) and there is a Marx Memorial Library and a Marx House in north-east London. But there seems little immediate prospect in the late twentieth century of Britain becoming a Marxist country. There is not even a large professedly Marxist party in Britain. The British Communist Party is minute in numbers; other Marxist parties are merely tiny sects; and although there have been Marxist influences on the Labour Party and the Trade Union movement, they have been exaggerated by both adherents and detractors. Indeed, Marxism has never been the dominant influence on the labour movement in Britain.

The English like to think of themselves as a pragmatic people. Marxism has seemed to most of them too theoretical and too ideological for their taste. They despise theory and ideology is foreign to them; literally, it is something for foreigners. Consequently, the English have scant respect for the intellectual and one of the most damning things they can say about anyone is 'that fellow is too clever by half'. And Marx himself had frequent occasion to complain that what the British really lacked was 'a socialist theory and a revolutionary temper'.

There are nonetheless two connections between Marx and England which are essential ingredients both in the story of his work as well as of his life and in the story of what has happened to his ideas after his death.

Firstly, Marx was living in London – proud, problem-ridden, growing

28, Dean Street, Soho, where the Marx family lived in two rooms on the top floor from 1850 to 1856

Victorian London, the centre of world development. London was then the biggest, the richest, the most liberal city in Europe with a deep-rooted tolerance for political exiles and a reformed police force which did not harass them all the time. As well as keeping up with his fellow-exiles from Europe and thus maintaining his revolutionary notions of politics and philosophy from pre-1848, Marx could now give these ideas an economic dimension inspired by his experience of the most advanced industrial country in the world. The rapid expansion of the railway network, the switch from wood to iron in ships, the growth and concentration of productive forces based on coal, iron and steel – all these made an even bigger impact on the popular mind of the mid-nineteenth century than do today's marvels of space travel and microtechnology. Marx was particularly excited by a model electric train on show in Regent Street. This impression of London as the headquarters of international capitalism and England as the workshop of the world were epitomised by what Marx called 'The Pantheon in the modern Rome' – the Great Exhibition held in the specially constructed Crystal Palace in 1851 – just two years after Marx's arrival in London.

Secondly, Marx's intellectual labours were greatly facilitated by the library in the British Museum which contained half a million books and the finest collection on economics in the world. If Englishmen were suspicious of intellectuals, intellectuals could always find a place to study there. A new

Reading Room was opened in 1855 and an exile from Italy, Antonio Panizzi, was in charge. Marx got his ticket in June 1850 and began avidly reading back numbers of the newly founded *Economist*. He would regularly arrive at nine in the morning and not leave until seven at night, occupying seat no. G-7, fifth on the right from the entrance and, typically, next to the reference section.

What Marx progressively unearthed in his long hours in the British Museum was the economic bedrock for his revolutionary theories. On leaving France, Marx had considered fresh revolutions in Europe to be imminent. A close study of the *Economist* slowed him down. 'A new revolution', he wrote, 'is possible only in consequence of a new crisis. It is, however, just as certain as this crisis'. In other words, to understand the dynamics of revolution, it was necessary to understand the dynamics of capitalist society, its economic law of motion – and Marx devoted the rest of his life to discovering it. Thus to the vision of dialectical conflict drawn from Hegel's philosophy and the revolutionary socialist politics drawn from France, Marx began to add the specifically English experience of capitalism in theory and practice.

For the theory of capitalism, Marx began to study the classical English economists. These writers were rather broader in their approach than present-day economists. They referred to their subject as 'political economy' and in fact produced theories that aimed at encompassing all social phenomena. Marx re-read Adam Smith whose *Wealth of Nations* published in 1776 was the Bible of *laissez-faire* economics. Smith welcomed intensified division of labour by which individuals were responsible for a smaller and smaller part of the production process, glorified in the pursuit of gain in a free market with no governmental interference, and was confident that a 'hidden hand' would ensure that the economic free-for-all would result in increased social wealth. But it was particularly David Ricardo whom Marx admired. Ricardo had called his study, in a famous phrase, 'an enquiry into the laws which determine the division of the produce of industry amongst the classes who concur in its formation'. The answer to this enquiry would reveal the class structure of society and explain the factors which governed capital accumulation. Ricardo had found the key to these questions in the view that labour was the source of all value and considered that a labour theory of value, if rigorously pursued, could provide a total explanation for the striking economic development of capitalism and also its possible stagnation. Although Marx did not share the political views of Smith and Ricardo, he admired their efforts to find a systematic, scientific account of the capitalist system. At the same time, Marx began to read the socialist disciples of Ricardo such as Thomas Hodgskin and John Bray. Just as there had been radical Hegelians, so there were radical Ricardians who began to ask why, if it was

The Reading Room at the British Museum where Marx found many of
the materials for his analysis of capitalism

labour that *produced* all value, should not labour also *receive* all value: were
not those who received huge incomes without contributing any labour in
fact redundant? The working class was not getting the full value of its
labour: the capitalist was expropriating it. Political economy pointed to class
conflict, not to social harmony. Although Marx considered their answers to
these questions unduly moralistic and utopian, he was beginning to see how
Ricardo could be used to predict the downfall of the capitalist system and its
replacement by socialism.

For as well as reading the economic theorists, Marx was also collecting a
good deal of empirical evidence. Much of this came free of charge from
journals and periodicals and official government reports – the famous Blue
Books – which collected evidence on prices, profits, wages and the processes
of production – how factories worked and how factory workers lived. Marx
learned what a potent force capitalism was as an engine of growth and how
badly the workers were doing out of it. But he learned also about how the
workers were not just a labour force but a new kind of working class, a
proletariat, and, as he thought, potential creators of a new order of society.
From the earliest days of what has been called the industrial revolution,
people in power feared the threat of another kind of revolution – a political

Above: Marx's reputed place in the Reading Room of the British Museum
Below: Marx's name and address on his application to renew his Reading
Room ticket

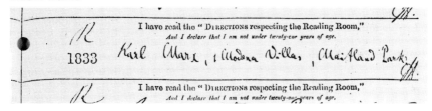

and social revolution. In the industrial north, workers had smashed machines
and gone on strike. But they had created new forms of organisation also,
which were new then but are now familiar – trade unions seeking to raise
wages and mass political movements pressing for a reform of Parliament
and for legislation to shorten the working day and to improve factory conditions. The 1840s was the decade of the Chartists, the first large-scale
independent working-class movement in history.

But Marx could not bring his economic studies to anything like com-
pletion. This was partly because he was still involved in the labyrinthine
intrigues of the refugee politics which centred on Soho. Marx had a foible
for constantly predicting the imminence of an economic crisis (and got
extremely angry when his friends pulled his leg about it), but he despised

his impetuous fellow-revolutionaries who had no time for serious economic analysis. He eventually left the Communist League, which was too full of hotheaded activists, and withdrew from active politics although he continued throughout the 1850s to be an assiduous and often sarcastic observer of the various machinations of the London refugees. Deprived of the possibility of engaging in national politics on their home ground, these refugees indulged in feverish political infighting in London. The result was a constantly changing kaleidoscope of plans, committees and alliances, not least among the largest group of refugees – the Germans, whose sects a bewildered Herzen compared in number to the forty times forty churches traditionally to be found in Moscow. Marx professed himself quite content with his new situation, writing to Engels:

> I am quite pleased with the public and genuine isolation in which we two, you and I find ourselves. It entirely suits our position and principles. We have now finished with the system of mutual concessions, with half truths admitted for reasons of propriety and with our duty of sharing in the public ridicule in the party with all these asses.

Nonetheless he continued to follow refugee politics with the closest attention and even wrote several bitingly ironic pamphlets on the subject.

More basic to Marx's difficulty in getting ahead with his work on economics were his domestic circumstances. On moving to Dean Street, Soho, the family was crowded into two rooms at the top of a terraced house, a sort of flat sub-let by a tenant. The house was built in the time of George II and is now part of a smart restaurant. In the 1850s this flat was not only cramped, it was without running water or sanitation. Water for drinking, cooking and washing had to be carried from the ground floor where the lavatory was also located. There was, however, some relief in the regular weekend trek to Hampstead Heath for an extended picnic accompanied by much recitation of Shakespeare. A hasty reading of Marx's correspondence gives the impression that Marx's family difficulties were largely due to their living in the most grinding poverty. Indeed, three of his children died prematurely. The following extract (from a letter to Engels in 1852) is not untypical:

> My wife is ill, little Jenny is ill, Lenchen has a sort of nervous fever, I cannot and could not call the doctor because I have no money for medicine. For 8–10 days I have fed the family on bread and potatoes of which it is still questionable whether I can rustle up any today. Naturally this diet was not recommended in the present climatic conditions. I did not write any articles for Dana, because I did not have the penny to go and read newspapers . . .

I had put off until the beginning of September all the creditors who, as you know, are only paid off in small sums. Now there is a general storm. I have tried everything, but in vain . . .

The best and most desirable thing that could happen would be that the landlady throw me out of the house. At least I would then be quit of the sum of £22. But I can scarcely trust her to be so obliging. Also baker, milkman, the man with the tea, greengrocer, old butcher's bills. How can I get clear of all this hellish muck? Finally in the last 8–10 days, I have borrowed some shillings and pence (this is the most fatal thing, but it was necessary to avoid perishing) from layabouts.

In fact, the Marx family were never poor by ordinary standards: their income even in the worst years was about three times that earned by an average skilled workman. Marx's difficulties were caused by his pride, his desire to keep up appearances and his almost total inability to manage his financial resources. Microeconomics were certainly not Marx's strongpoint.

Marx never had any paid employment. He did once try for a job as a railway clerk but was turned down because of his atrocious handwriting. But he did enjoy an income of sorts in the 1850s as London correspondent of the influential *New York Daily Tribune*. Partly owing to the background information provided by the British Museum, Marx's contributions had considerable depth and a wealth of hard fact. Apart from his almost pathological hatred of Russia, his pieces were much appreciated and he was, in the words of the *Tribune*'s editor, 'not only one of the most highly valued, but one of the best-paid contributors attached to the journal'. Marx's own opinion, however, was less complimentary: 'the continual newspaper muck' was how he referred to his journalism. 'Purely scientific works', he wrote, 'are something completely different.'

In the genesis of these 'purely scientific works' it is difficult to underestimate the contribution of Friedrich Engels. At a mundane level, Engels was of immense material assistance to Marx; he supported the Marx family regularly with money. This was often conveyed in the form of banknotes torn in half and sent in two separate envelopes for safety. It has been calculated that Engels gave Marx more than £100,000 in present-day values. He also initially wrote the articles for the *New York Daily Tribune* which Marx (whose English was not good enough) sent off in his own name. He even apparently accepted the paternity of Marx's illegitimate son, only revealing the truth on his death-bed.

But Engels was much more than the paymaster of the Marx family. He also introduced Marx to another aspect of the English connection – the very different atmosphere of Manchester in the North, the thrusting city at the

Engels and Marx with Marx's daughters Laura, Eleanor and Jenny in 1864

centre of an industrial region which looked to it as a provincial capital – Cottonopolis, Manchester was the shock city of the mid-nineteenth century which people of all varieties visited like a Mecca to understand what was happening and what would happen in the future. It even had a school of economic thought named after it. Many feared that Manchester would be the crucible of revolution, a prospect of course welcomed by Marx and Engels. Engels had already written his book entitled *The Condition of the Working Classes in England* which was a study of the social impact of industrialisation and a pioneering work in the relatively modern fields of urban geography and sociology. In his portrayal a major role was allotted to the Manchester-Salford conurbation which contained almost half a million people and formed the major industrial district of England. Its wealth was centred on the cotton trade, in which about a third of its population was directly employed. Engels produced his effect by a vivid attention to detail, of which the following extract is a typical example. Describing that bit of Manchester known as Little Ireland, Engels wrote:

> Masses of refuse, offal, and sickening filth lie among standing pools in all directions; the atmosphere is poisoned by the effluvia from these, and laden and darkened by the smoke of a dozen tall factory chimneys. A hoard of ragged women and children swarm about here, as filthy as the swine that thrive upon the garbage heaps and in the puddles. In short the whole rookery furnishes such a hateful and repulsive spectacle as can be hardly equalled in the worst court of the Irk. The race that lives in these ruinous cottages, behind broken windows, mended with oilskin, sprung doors, and rotten door-posts, or in dark, wet cellars, in measureless filth and stench, in this atmosphere penned in as if with a purpose, this race must really have reached the lowest stage of humanity.

And his general conclusion was that

> the working class of the great cities offers a graduated scale of conditions in life, in the best cases a temporarily endurable existence for hard work and good wages, good and endurable, that is, from the workers' standpoint; in the worst cases, bitter want reaching even homelessness and death by starvation. The average is much nearer the worst cases than the best.

Engels then went on to describe the results accruing from these conditions. He detailed the diseases, particularly consumption, that produced 'pale, emaciated, narrow-chested and hollow-eyed ghosts'. (In Manchester more than half the children of working-class parents died before the age of five.) He described the illiteracy that had its counterpart in bigotry and fanaticism, and the alcoholism that fostered sexual immorality and ever-increasing crime. There followed an account of the factory system with its exploitation of women and children as cheap labour, and its spate of accidents and spinal injuries. Engels particularly emphasised the power of the mill owners over their operatives in everything from sexual favours to rent and the price of food in the factory-owned shops.

Engels made excellent use in his survey of government statistics (much as

Marx did in writing *Capital*). His description of the working class was embedded in an analysis of the evolution of industrial capitalism which lent it a coherent historical and conceptual framework. He stressed the significance of the drive to larger and larger businesses, the reserve army of the unemployed that could be called on in time of expansion, and the regular occurrence of crises. And the simple prognostication was clear: 'The war of the poor against the rich will be the most bloodthirsty the world has ever seen. It is particularly easy to forecast future events in England because in that country every aspect of social development is so plain and clear cut. The revolution must come . . .'

For all that he viewed Manchester as the crucible of revolution, life there was for Engels a kind of mini-exile. He agreed with the Chartist leader Harney that it would be better 'to be hanged in London than die naturally in Manchester'. Engels had moved there in 1850, driven mainly by financial pressure, to take up a position as senior clerk in the German-based firm of Ermen and Engels of which his father was a partner. It employed about eight hundred people and manufactured sewing thread. The move to Manchester was regarded by Engels as temporary but he was to remain there for two decades. His life was essentially a double one: the days were spent in the office, the evenings and weekends devoted to writing political articles, studying military science (in which he became so adept that he earned himself the nickname of 'General'), and mastering some twenty foreign languages. Although he found the office work monotonous and time-consuming, Engels ironically proved a good businessman and his position and status grew in importance. By 1854 he had become a member of the Manchester Cotton Exchange and enjoyed an annual salary plus a share in the profits that brought his annual income by the end of the 1850s to about £20,000 in present-day terms. On the death of his father in 1860, Engels negotiated an agreement which actually gave him a partnership. He allowed himself to be bought out in 1870 and by the end of his life was, again in present-day values, a millionaire.

Engels enjoyed an active social life. He maintained two establishments: bachelor lodgings near the city centre where he entertained his business friends and a house in the outskirts where he lived with Mary Burns, an Irish working-class girl whom he had got to know on his first visit to the city. Engels went in for several of the activities beloved of the Manchester bourgeoisie: he attended the concerts founded by another German emigré, Charles Hallé; he bought a fine stallion and rode regularly with the Cheshire Hunt; and he was a prominent member of two prosperous clubs – the Albert Club and the Schiller Institute – eventually becoming chairman of the latter. He maintained a wide circle of friends in Manchester, including Dr

Gumpert, a distinguished pediatrician, Samuel Moore, a barrister who was to translate *Capital* into English, and Karl Schorlemmer, who held the first English chair in organic chemistry. And in this sort of life Marx shared by proxy. Marx and Engels corresponded several times a week. Marx visited Manchester frequently during the year, once staying for three months to avoid his creditors. Engels was an invaluable informant about the movement of the markets and the actual workings of a capitalist enterprise.

With the rise in Engels's fortunes, Marx's life, too, began to improve. Increasing gifts from Engels were augmented by a substantial legacy and a loan which Marx managed to squeeze out of his wife's Dutch uncle Lion Philips, founder of the giant Philips electrical company. (Ironically, Philips now represents late twentieth-century capitalism – large scale, multinational, science based, with specialised management: Marx's capitalism was carboniferous – based on coal and iron and steam power – and centred on textiles.) The family moved to a four storey terraced house in the newly developing suburb of Kentish Town where expenses were proportionately higher. The elder children attended what Marx referred to as a 'ladies seminary' and had private lessons in French, Italian, drawing and music. Marx's mother was said to have complained that she wished Karl would *make* a bit of capital instead of just writing about it: but he was as resolved as ever 'to pursue my aim through thick and thin and not let bourgeois society turn me into a money-making machine'. But he was surprised at the financial difficulties that his attitude entailed. 'It is astonishing', he remarked naïvely to Engels, 'how lack of income together with debts that are never completely cleared blows up the old shit in spite of all assistance in minor matters.' Nevertheless, two large legacies in 1864, together with Engels's partnership enabled Marx to get down to writing his *magnum opus*.

Like Darwin with *The Origin of Species*, Marx is known as the author of a single book – *Das Kapital*. This is in some ways a pity as Marx did write many more accessible works – the splendid historical sweep of the beginning of *The German Ideology*, for instance, or the brilliant political pamphlets on Louis Napoleon. And Marx's *Capital* does have the reputation for being a difficult book. Several socialist politicians have tried to sustain a reputation as plain, down-to-earth people by declaring that they tried to read *Capital* but gave up very quickly when they came across a page where the footnote was longer than the text. On the other hand, the only review to appear in English (Marx wrote in German and an English translation did not appear for twenty years) declared that 'the author's views may be as pernicious as we conceive them to be, but there can be no question as to the plausibility of his logic, the vigour of his rhetoric, and the charm with which he invests the driest problems of political economy'.

Marx in 1866, a year before the publication of *Das Kapital*

In fact, *Capital* is a book with two halves to it. The first sections are rather abstract and some of the concepts unfamiliar – though not half as obscure as some of the commentaries devoted to it! This is because Marx's approach was quite familiar to economists in the mid-nineteenth century but thereafter abandoned by the orthodox schools of economics. Since the third quarter of the nineteenth century, economists in Western Europe and America have tended to look at the capitalist system as given, construct models of it, assuming private property, profit and a more or less free market, and to discuss the functionings of this model, concentrating particularly on prices. This 'marginalist' school of economics has no concept of value apart from price. To Marx, this procedure seemed superficial for two reasons: firstly, he considered it superficial in a literal sense, in that it was only a description of phenomena lying on the surface of capitalist society without an analysis of the mode of production that gave rise to these phenomena. Secondly, this approach took the capitalist system for granted whereas Marx wished to analyse 'the birth, life and death of a given social organism and its replacement by another, superior order'.

In order to achieve these two aims, Marx took over the concepts of the 'classical' economists that were still the generally accepted tool of economic analysis, and used them to draw very different conclusions. Ricardo had made a distinction between use-value and exchange-value. The exchange-value of an object was something separate from its price and consisted of the amount of labour embodied in the objects produced, though Ricardo thought that the price in fact tended to approximate to the exchange-value. Thus – in opposition to later analyses – the value of an object was determined by the circumstances of production rather than those of demand. Marx took over these concepts, but, in his attempt to show that capitalism was not static but a historically relative system of class exploitation, supplemented Ricardo's view by introducing the idea of surplus-value, the idea that Engels thought was Marx's principal 'discovery' in economics. Surplus-value was defined as the difference between the value of the products of labour and the cost of producing that labour-power, i.e. the labourer's subsistence; for the exchange-value of labour-power was equal to the amount of labour necessary to reproduce that labour-power and this was normally much lower than the exchange-value of the products of that labour-power. The essential point was that the capitalist got the worker to work longer than was merely sufficient to embody in his product the value of his labour-power: if the labour-power of the worker (roughly what it cost to keep him alive and fit) was £4 a day and the worker could embody £4 of value in the product on which he was working in eight hours: then, if he worked ten hours, the last two hours would yield surplus value – in this case £1. It was this rate of surplus value around which the struggle between workers and capitalists centred. And in the long run the rate of surplus value, and so profit was bound to decline. Put very simply, Marx's reason for thinking that the rate of profit would decrease was that, with the introduction of machinery, there would be less labour time to be exploited, thus yielding less surplus value. Of course, machinery would increase production and colonial markets would absorb some of the surplus, but these were only palliatives and an eventual crisis was inevitable.

The second half of *Capital* contained a description of the historical genesis of capitalism which is at times extremely readable. It was here particularly that Marx made pioneering use of the official statistical information that came to be available from the middle of the nineteenth century onwards. Readers who find the beginning of *Capital* too arid would do well to follow Marx's advice to Mrs Kugelmann, a friend of the family, and begin by reading chapters such as that on 'The Working Day' where Marx described in detail the physical and mental degradation forced on men, women and children by working long hours in unhealthy conditions and related the bitter struggle to gain some relief by legal limits on the number of hours worked and the passing of factory acts. He continued his indictment of capitalism in the chapter on 'Machinery and Modern Industry' describing the crippling effect of machinery on workers and the environmental effects of capitalist exploitation of agriculture. But the masterpiece of the book is undoubtedly the long final section on 'Capitalist Accumulation'. The capitalist, being a prey to 'a Faustian conflict between the passion for accumulation and the desire for enjoyment', was forced to create an 'industrial reserve army' or vast pool of temporarily unemployed workers to serve the fluctuations of the market. Marx brought together the different strands of his analyses in the thundering denunciation:

We saw, when analysing the production of relative surplus-value: within the capitalist system all methods for raising the social productiveness of labour are brought about at the cost of the individual labourer; all means for the development of production transform themselves into means of domination over, and exploitation of, the producers; they mutilate the labourer into a fragment of a man, degrade him to the level of an appendage of a machine, destroy every remnant of charm in his work and turn it into a hated toil; they estrange from him the intellectual potentialities of the labour-process in the same proportion as science is incorporated in it as an independent power; they distort the conditions under which he works, subject him during the labour-process to a despotism the more hateful for its meanness; they transform his life-time into working-time, and drag his wife and child beneath the wheels of the Juggernaut of capital.

But all methods for the production of surplus-value are at the same time methods of accumulation; and every extension of accumulation becomes again a means for the development of those methods. It follows therefore that in proportion as capital accumulates, the lot of the labourer, be his payment high or low, must grow worse. The law, finally, that always equilibrates the relative surplus-population, or industrial reserve army, to the extent and energy of accumulation, this law rivets the labourer to capital more firmly than the wedges of Vulcan did Prometheus to the rock. It establishes an accumulation of misery, corresponding with accumulation of capital. Accumulation of wealth at one pole is, therefore, at the same time accumulation of misery, agony of toil, slavery, ignorance, brutality, mental degradation, at the opposite pole, i.e. on the side of the class that produces its own product in the form of capital.

This judgement was supported by a series of detailed studies, moving yet objective, on the condition of the British working classes over the previous twenty years, the British agricultural proletariat, and the misery of Ireland.

But Marx's conclusion was nevertheless optimistic. For the theory of surplus-value had implications for the long-term future of capitalism. These were: for the capitalists, that their rate of profit would decline; for the workers, that their relative standard of living would decrease; and for the capitalist system as a whole, that it would be shaken by a series of crises that would culminate in a transition to communism, a new classless society in which all human beings would have their needs met. Marx saw a strong element of continuity between capitalism and communism. He talked, for example, of share capital as 'the most perfect form of capital leading to communism' and referred to the joint stock company as a sort of communism within capitalism. There was thus a striking contrast between the increasingly social character of the capitalist process of production and the anti-social character of capitalist private property – a contrast which in itself summed up Marx's basic critique of capitalism. It was this thought which underlay the famous passage with which Marx rounded off his work:

Along with the constantly diminishing number of the magnates of capital, who usurp and monopolise all advantages of this process of transformation, grows the mass of misery, oppression, slavery, degradation, exploitation: but with this too grows the revolt of the working class, a class always increasing in numbers, and disciplined, united, organised by the very mechanism of the process of capitalist production itself. The monopoly of capital becomes a fetter upon the mode of production, which has sprung up and flourished along with, and under it. Centralisation of the means of production and socialisation of labour at last reach a point where they become incompatible with their capitalist integument. This integument is burst asunder. The knell of capitalist private property sounds. The expropriators are expropriated.

Marx was quite right in his forecast that *Capital* would not pay for the cigars he smoked while writing it. His wife wrote rather bitterly to a friend: 'you can believe me that seldom has a book been written under more difficult circumstances, and I could write a secret history that would uncover an infinite amount of worry, trouble and anxiety. If the workers had an inkling of the sacrifice that was necessary to complete this work, written only for them and in their interest, they would perhaps show a bit more interest'. It took four long years for the first printing of a thousand copies to be sold and most of the reviews that appeared were actually written by the indefatigable Engels. Marx was very disappointed that an English translation did not appear in his lifetime. It began to look doubtful whether, as Marx had vowed, the bourgeoisie really would be made to pay for the boils that had plagued him while writing it. Curiously – and prophetically – the first translation was into Russian, a country Marx had formerly dismissed simply as a bastion of reaction but in which he now became increasingly interested.

While writing *Capital*, Marx had re-entered the world of active politics after an absence of more than a decade. He was a leading figure in what came to be known as the First International. This 'International' (there were at least three subsequent ones) was a peculiarly loose and hybrid or-ganisation, the core of whose membership was formed by British trade unions. Thus its history marks the first stage in the turbulent and abiding saga of the relationship of Marxism, which envisages a thorough-going transformation of society, to the trade union movement which aims at the more accessible goals of improved wages and working conditions.

By the early 1860s, political and economic conditions were encouraging a revival of working-class activity in Europe. In England the successful struggle of the building workers for a nine-hour day encouraged the growth of or-ganised trade unions and the establishment in 1860 of the London Trade Council. In France, Napoleon III had begun to relax the anti-trade union laws in the hope of using the workers as a counterweight to the increasingly liberal opposition. A public meeting in London's Covent Garden in Sep-tember 1864 decided to establish an International Workingmen's Association and elected a General Council of thirty-four members, one of whom was Marx. He was also deputed to draw up an *Address to the Working Class*. In contrast to the *Communist Manifesto*, the *Address* contained no sweeping generalisations or appeals to revolutionary action. It began with the state-ment that 'it is a great fact that the misery of the working masses has not diminished from 1848 to 1864' and proceeded to document this from official statistics. Thus there had to be an end to rule by capitalists and 'to conquer political power has become the great duty of the working classes'. In this enterprise Marx started from the principle (often neglected subsequently) that 'the emancipation of the working classes must be achieved by the working classes themselves'.

Marx had no difficulty in establishing his ascendancy in the General Council as he could act as intermediary between the English and the continentals. He also attributed his dominance to German ideological superiority and the fact that the rest of the Council felt 'German Science' to be 'very useful and even indispensable'. The carefully kept minute books of the International (Englishmen are very good minute keepers) have a remarkably up-to-date look about them: British policy towards Ireland and the Fenian rebels, forerunners of the IRA, the independence of Russian-dominated Poland and the struggle for the eight-hour day were high on the agenda. The importance and size of the International were, understandably, grossly exaggerated by the governments of Europe. Its main strength lay in practical matters such as mutual financial support for strikes and the prevention of importing black-leg labour.

The eventual downfall of the International was caused by the most exciting political event of Marx's lifetime – the uprising known as the Paris Commune, after which all the current Communist Parties are named. This took place in the aftermath of the Franco-Prussian war of 1870. The Emperor Napoleon had been defeated and captured at the battle of Sedan and the victorious Prussians ringed Paris with their troops while negotiating a settlement with the new provisional government headed by Thiers. The establishment of the Commune was not the result of any preconceived plan, but of the void left in Paris when Thiers withdrew all government officials, local and central, to Versailles. This left the Central Committee of the National Guard as the only body capable of exercising effective control. The Central Committee immediately instituted direct elections by manhood suffrage to create a popular assembly which on 28 March 1871 gave itself the name *Commune de Paris* after the title of the Council set up during the French Revolution in 1792. For there is tradition even in revolution.

Marx had an ambivalent attitude to the Commune whose actual measures were not particularly socialist. In fact, the Commune had such a short life, was composed of such disparate elements and operated under such exceptional circumstances that it is difficult to ascribe any coherent policy to it. After the Commune had been in existence for two months, Thiers did a deal with the Prussians and marched into Paris with regular troops who massacred some twenty thousand of their opponents. The last stand of the Communards was

Scene in the Père-Lachaise Cemetery, Paris, following the massacre of
the defenders of the Paris Commune in May 1871

in the giant Père-Lachaise cemetery where they were forced to retreat from
tombstone to tombstone until, herded together in a corner, they were shot
down below a wall which still bears their memorial.

Faced with such a blood bath, Marx discarded his previous reservations.
French politics were, in any case, far more exciting than British or German,
and Marx had intimate connections with France: two of his daughters had
married Frenchmen. The rise of Louis Napoleon after the 1848 revolution
had called forth his best political journalism. Now once again he rose to the
occasion and produced on behalf of the General Council a brilliant celebration
and defence of the ideals of the Commune.

Marx's pamphlet on the Commune shows him as a master of political
invective. Consider, for example, this portrait of the new French President,
Adolphe Thiers:

> A master in small state roguery, a virtuoso in perjury and treason, a
> craftsman in all the petty stratagems, cunning devices, and base perfidies
> of parliamentary party-warfare; never scrupling, when out of office, to
> fan a revolution, and to stifle it in blood when at the helm of the state;
> with class prejudices standing him in the place of ideas, and vanity in the
> place of a heart; his private life as infamous as his public life is odious –

even now when playing the part of a French Sulla, he cannot help setting off the abomination of his deeds by the ridicule of his ostentation.

More importantly, Marx considered the Commune to have been a model of the sort of government for which a socialist revolution should strive. As such, it deserves lengthy quotation as it was to be the kind of political model on which the original Russian Soviets were based. Marx wrote:

> The Commune was to be the political form of even the smallest country hamlet, and in the rural districts the standing army was to be replaced by a national militia, with an extremely short term of service. The rural communes of every district were to administer their common affairs by an assembly of delegates in the central town, and these district assemblies were again to send deputies to the National Delegation in Paris, each delegate to be at any time revocable and bound by the *mandat imperatif* (formal instructions) of his constituents. The few but important functions which still would remain for a central government were not to be suppressed, as has been intentionally mis-stated, but were to be discharged by Communal, and therefore strictly responsible agents. The unity of the nation was not to be broken, but, on the contrary, to be organised by the Communal Constitution and to become a reality by the destruction of the State power which claimed to be the embodiment of that unity independent of, and superior to, the nation itself, from which it was but a parasitic excrescence. . . Instead of deciding once in three or six years which member of the ruling class was to misrepresent the people in Parliament, universal suffrage was to serve the people, constituted in Communes, as individual suffrage serves every other employer in the search for the workmen and managers in his business. And it is well known that companies, like individuals, in matters of real business, generally know how to put the right man in the right place, and, if they for once make a mistake, to redress it promptly. On the other hand, nothing could be more foreign to the spirit of the Commune than to supersede universal suffrage by hierarchic investiture.

The story of the Commune has entered socialist mythology. Marx wrote that 'Working men's Paris, with its Commune, will be for ever celebrated as the glorious harbinger of a new society. The martyrs are enshrined in the great heart of the working class. Its exterminators history has already nailed to that eternal pillory from which all the prayers of their priests will not avail to redeem them.'

Lenin evoked the Commune as a model for the 1917 revolution; and the first Russian sputnik took a piece of a Commune flag into space. It also

ANNIVERSARY of the SOCIAL REVOLUTION

OF THE 18th OF MARCH, 1871.

A PUBLIC MEETING

WILL BE HELD IN

ST. GEORGE'S HALL,

LANGHAM PLACE, REGENT STREET,

UNDER THE AUSPICES OF THE

Members of the International, the Democrats of London,
and the Refugees of the Commune,

ON MONDAY, MARCH 18, 1872,

AT EIGHT P.M., TO COMMEMORATE THE

SOCIAL REVOLUTION OF PARIS.

President - **CITIZEN JUNG.**
Vice-Presidents { ,, **RANVIER.**
{ ,, **HALES.**

FRENCH SPEAKERS:
RANVIER, Member of the Commune
LISSAGARAY, National Guard
LONGUET, Member of the Commune
VAILLANT
THEISZ
LEO FRANKEL   Members
SERRAILLIER   of the
ANDRIEUX   Commune
ARNAUD
DELAHAYE, Member of the Labour
   Committee
COURNET, Member of the Commune
CAMELINAT, Director of the Mint
EUDES, Member of the Commune
JOFFRIN, Delegate from the 18th
   Arrondisement

LE MOUSSU, Commissary of Public
   Safety
BOURSIER, Member of the Central
   Committee

ENGLISH SPEAKERS:

DR. KARL MARX
HALES
MILNER
WESTON
McDONNELL
JOHNSON
BOON
MITCHELL
BRADNICK

Poster advertising an anniversary commemoration of the Commune and featuring Marx as a speaker

made Marx notorious. His pamphlet, he wrote, 'is making the devil of a noise and I have the honour to be at this moment the most threatened and abused man in London. That really does me good after the tedious twenty-year idyll in my den!' The London *Daily Telegraph* and the *New York Herald* hastened to interview the Red Terrorist Doctor. But, for all its public impact, the International after the Commune was a spent force.

What finally killed it was the split between the supporters of Marx and those led by the Russian anarchist Bakunin. The political situation in Europe after the Commune tended to sharpen the differences between Marx and Bakunin: Marx gradually gave up expecting a quick revolution and was unwilling to have the International committed to the support of spasmodic risings in Italy, Spain and Russia – the countries chiefly susceptible to anarchist doctrines. The anarchists seemed to consider any revolutionary uprising to be justified as a step towards the total destruction of contemporary society. To them the General Council was an authoritarian irrelevance. Anarchism has always been (and continues to be) a thorn in the flesh of Marxism and the following dialogue shows why. It is reconstructed from notes that Marx scribbled in the margin of a copy of one of Bakunin's works:

BAKUNIN: What does it mean to say that the proletariat is organised as a ruling class?

MARX: It means that the proletariat, instead of fighting piecemeal against the economically privileged classes, has obtained enough strength and organisation to use general means of forcibly expressing itself in this struggle; but it can only use economic means which abolish its own character as wage-labourers, that is as a class; with its complete victory, therefore, its domination is at an end because its character as a class has disappeared.

BAKUNIN: Will, perhaps, the whole of the proletariat be at the head of the government?

MARX: In a trade union, for example, is the executive committee composed of the whole of the union? Will all division of labour and the different functions that it entails disappear? And in Bakunin's construction from the bottom to the top will everyone be at the top? Then there will be no bottom. Will all members of the Commune manage the common interests of the enterprise at the same time? Then there is no distinction between enterprise and commune.

BAKUNIN: There are about forty million Germans. Will, for example, all the forty million be members of the government?

MARX: Certainly! For the thing begins with the self-government of the Commune.

BAKUNIN: The whole people will govern and there will be no one to be governed.

MARX: According to this principle, when a man rules himself, he does not rule himself; since he is only himself and no one else.

BAKUNIN: Then there will be no government, no State, but if there is a State in existence there will also be governors and slaves.

MARX: This merely means: when class rule has disappeared, there will no longer be any State in the present political sense of the word. . .

BAKUNIN: Universal suffrage by the whole people of representatives and rulers of the State – this is the last word of the Marxists as well as of the democratic school. They are lies behind which lurks the despotism of a governing minority, lies all the more dangerous in that this minority appears as the expression of the so-called people's will.

MARX: Under collective property, the so-called will of the people disappears in order to make way for the real will of the co-operative.

BAKUNIN: Result: rule of the great majority of the people by a privileged minority. But, the Marxists say, this minority will consist of workers. Yes, indeed, but of ex-workers, who, once they become only representatives or rulers of the people, cease to be workers.

MARX: No more than a manufacturer today ceases to be a capitalist when he becomes a member of the municipal council.

BAKUNIN: And from the heights of the State they begin to look down upon the whole common world of the workers. From that time on they represent not the people but themselves and their own claims to govern the people. Those who can doubt this know nothing at all about human nature.

MARX: If Mr Bakunin were in the know, if only with the position of a manager in a workers' co-operative, he would send all his nightmares about authority to the devil. He should have asked himself: what form can administrative function assume on the basis of that workers' state, if it pleases him to call it thus? . . .

This exchange brings out the abiding problem of Marxism as a movement of political revolution: how to prevent a gap opening up between leaders and led and the concentration, rather than the diffusion, of political power.

The final Congress of the International was held in The Hague in 1872. The figure of Marx attracted much public attention: his black broadcloth suit contrasted with his white hair and beard and he would screw a monocle into his eye when he wanted to scrutinise his audience. In order to prevent the General Council falling into the hands of the Bakuninists, Engels proposed that its seat be transferred to New York where it soon lost all momentum.

Marx did have a real, if tenuous, connection with the United States. Both he and Engels had seriously contemplated emigrating to America in the 1850s; and Engels did actually visit New England in 1888. As well as writing for the *New York Daily Tribune*, Marx followed events in the United States, particularly the Civil War, with great interest. He even drafted a message from the General Council to Abraham Lincoln addressing him as 'the single-minded son of the working class'. America was, of course, the supreme haven for refugees and indigent emigrants. Many of Marx's closest German friends settled there for good.

But Marx himself remained in England and was increasingly dogged by ill health. He desperately tried to complete further volumes of *Capital* but only left a mass of manuscripts. It fell to Engels to put this material in order and publish two further volumes. We have a glimpse of Marx towards the end of his life that we owe to the Empress Victoria, wife of the German Emperor Frederick III and eldest daughter of Queen Victoria. The Empress was apparently interested in Marx and asked the Liberal MP Sir Mountstuart Grant Duff to find out about him. Grant Duff immediately asked Marx to lunch at his club and subsequently reported to the Empress as follows:

He is a short, rather small man with grey hair and beard which contrasts strangely with a still dark moustache. The face is somewhat round; the forehead well shaped and filled up – the eyes rather hard, but the whole expression pleasant rather than not, by no means that of a gentleman who is in the habit of eating babies in their cradles – which is I daresay the view which the police take of him. His talk was that of a well-informed, nay learned man – much interested in Comparative Grammar which had led him into the old Slavonic and other out-of-the-way studies and was varied by many quaint turns and little dry bits of humour . . . It was all very *positif*, slightly cynical, without any appearance of enthusiasm – interesting and often, as I thought, showing very correct ideas when conversing on the past and the present, but vague and unsatisfactory when he turned to the future.

They talked for three hours – of Russia where Marx expected 'a great but not distant crash' and of Germany where there seemed to him a strong possibility of mutiny in the army. Marx further explained that the revolution could be a very long term affair. Grant Duff's general conclusion was: 'It will not be Marx who, whether he wishes it or not, will turn the world upside down.'

During the last years of his life, enjoying a comfortable annual income from Engels, Marx's lifestyle became increasingly that of a Victorian gentleman. Of his three surviving children, the elder two married French socialist politicians – for they all shared the political passions of their father. Jenny, the eldest and in many ways the most attractive, married Charles Longuet and died from cancer a few months before her father, desperately worn out by the birth in rapid succession of six children. Laura's three children died in infancy and she herself committed suicide in 1912 together with her husband Paul Lafargue. Eleanor, the youngest, never married, threw herself energetically into the struggles of the labour movement and lived for several years with Edward Aveling, a dishonest sponger, openly unfaithful to her, who eventually drove her to suicide.

But the grim fate of his children was as yet in the future. In search of health, Marx made regular visits to fashionable spas such as Karlsbad and even spent two sad months in Algiers. When his wife Jenny died in 1881, Engels realised that this was Marx's own death warrant. His last trip was to Ventnor on the Isle of Wight. Here he was looked after by the same doctor who also attended the young Winston Churchill. In his last known letter, never made public, he tells his doctor that he has just learned of the death of his eldest daughter Jenny. 'Physical pain', he says, 'is the only stunner of mental pain.' He died in London on 14 March 1883, in his armchair. It was Engels who made the speech at his graveside:

> Marx was before all else a revolutionist. His real mission was to contribute . . . to the overthrow of capitalist society and the state institutions it has brought into being, to contribute to the liberation of the modern proletariat. His name will endure through the ages, and so also will his work.

Engels mentioned Siberia and California as places where Marx's work was already known but he said curiously little about England itself. England was, in fact, a less dynamic country than it had been thirty years before, and businessmen were facing increasingly severe competition from overseas countries which were going through their own industrial revolutions – particularly Germany and the United States. There were a few signs, indeed, that the British were beginning to face unprecedented problems. Nevertheless, the decade of Marx's death saw a significant upthrust in the British labour movement. There were street disturbances and even riots in London; trade unionism grew in strength and spread to unskilled labour; there were great strikes such as the dockers' strike of 1889. But the fact that Marx had lived and worked for more than thirty years in Britain did little to help the implantation of his ideas on the British left. Although socialism as a whole was growing in popularity, it was also divided. Marxism might appeal to prominent intellectuals such as William Morris, but the only Marxist party – the Social Democratic Federation led by Henry Hyndman – had little more than a thousand members. The Independent Labour Party,

The last known photograph of Marx, taken in Algiers in 1882

formed by Keir Hardie and his friends in 1893, avoided ideas of revolution and class confrontation and embodied a more ethical, non-conformist approach to socialism. In Britain, unlike the continent, socialism and religion were not seen as incompatible. R.H. Tawney's brand of Christian socialism was a strong influence on the Labour Party, which sprang from the Labour Representation Committee formed at the instigation of the TUC in 1900 and grew immensely in the pre-war years. But, again unlike other working parties on the continent, it was staunchly anti-Marxist in outlook. The attitude of many trade union leaders to Marx was summed up by the remark of Peter Fox on receiving a present from Marx of a copy of *Capital* – he felt like a man who had been given an elephant and did not know what to do with it. A few years before his death Marx himself considered that the British working class had sunk so low that they were no more than 'the tail of the great Liberal Party, i.e. their enslavers, the capitalists'. And it is not surprising that his last recorded words on Britain were 'To the devil with the British!'

Nor was the labour movement in Britain as international in its outlook as its continental counterparts. Indeed, it was less international than the capitalism of the period, which looked increasingly to profits from overseas markets – inside and outside the Empire – and less to those from investment at home. For capitalism itself was changing. As Marx had foreseen, bigger industrial units and new technology were increasing the tendency to monopoly. But the whole phenomenon of imperialist expansion in the late nineteenth century with the increasing role of finance capitalism managed by the Bank of England and the City together with the growing standard of living of at least most of the working class seemed to demand a new interpretation.

Without doubt the most influential new interpretation was that supplied by the Russian Lenin. Lenin, too, had a connection with England. He came to London on several occasions, visited Marx's old haunts, and even edited a revolutionary newspaper entitled *Iskra* (*The Spark*) in Clerkenwell Green. In London, too, took place the famous congress of the Russian Marxists where Lenin forced a split between Bolsheviks and Mensheviks. Like Marx, Lenin too drew a lot of his material for his theories of imperialism from Britain – material which helped to turn his 'spark' into a huge conflagration very different from anything envisaged by Marx.

3
THE REVOLUTIONARIES

People who *made* a revolution always see the day after
that they had no idea what they were doing, that the
revolution *made* does not in the least resemble the one
they would like to make. This is what Hegel calls the
irony of history, an irony which few historical
personalities can escape.

Engels

The spark lit by Lenin started a fire that led to many parts of the world. But
as the fire cooled, it became clear that it had often given rise to large con-
gealed structures in the shape of modern Communist Parties whose task
it has been to institutionalise Utopia. These Communist Parties are the
children of Lenin rather than of Marx. They form a kind of international
freemasonry. They enjoy a common language across international frontiers,
though one which is riddled with jargon, code words and covert allusions.
They provide a career structure offering material security and good promotion prospects. Communists may work through trade union front organisations that they control in varying degrees, but the supremacy of the Party
(witness recent events in Poland) is sacred. The two most striking characteristics of Communist Parties are their bureaucracy, from the tiniest cells to
the Politburo itself, and their hierarchy whereby power is extremely concentrated and moves downwards from the top.

The modern idea of a revolutionary party goes back to the Jacobins of
the French Revolution. They were originally a relatively liberal debating
association called The Society of Friends of Constitutions and got the name
Jacobin because they met in a convent in the rue des Jacobins in Paris.
During the course of the French Revolution they turned into a rigid, highly
centralised organisation of strict ideological purity backed up by frequent
use of the guillotine. This trend was carried on in France during the nineteenth century by Blanqui who was constantly in and out of prison for his
attempts at revolutionary *coups*. Apart from a brief flirtation in the aftermath of the 1848 revolution, Marx himself had had little time for Blanqui.
Indeed there is little about the idea of a party in Marx. He was caught
between two political worlds: he regarded the tactics of Blanqui as belong-

ing to an infantile, underdeveloped sort of socialism that pre-dated the arrival of a mass proletariat. At the same time, Marx did not have to deal with the mass political parties of capitalist democracy which developed after his death. This is because the modern political party in Western Europe owes its rise to the extension of the suffrage and the granting of power to an elected parliament, trends which only became pronounced late in Marx's life. The Second Reform Bill in England, which gave the vote to male householders, was passed in 1867. Similarly, the French Third Republic which followed the Commune was based on an electorate running into millions, as was also the German Reichstag. So naturally an effective organisation was needed to get the vote out and secure a parliamentary majority. But a party bent on electoral success was one thing; revolution, as Lenin knew, was quite another.

And Russia did not, at first glance, seem to be a promising place for Marxist revolution. The accepted view of Marxists everywhere was that the revolution would come first to Germany. Germany was an advanced industrialised nation, and German capitalism had already created the industrial proletariat necessary for revolution. The German workers were educated and politically mature, and they had survived repression. By 1900 they had built a large and powerful party organisation. There were more differences of opinion within it than there were in twentieth-century Communist Parties and there were socialists who claimed to be revising what Marx had said. But the party was highly efficient, like most things in Germany at that time, or since. In Russia, by contrast, there had been the energetic efforts at modernisation by Peter the Great and Catherine. But throughout the nineteenth century Russia was still a by-word for backwardness and political repression. The tide of Western liberalism had not penetrated Russia: popular participation in government, independent economic activity, separation of Church and State – these were all unknown. Moreover, Russia only really became part of Europe in the eighteenth century. Many educated Russians had a highly ambivalent attitude to the 'benefits' of European civilisation and saw Russia's past as supplying her with a special identity that they did not wish to see eclipsed. Thus even after the emancipation of the serfs in 1861, Russia continued to be an under-developed agrarian society controlled by a growing bureaucracy similar to that of France in the century before the revolution of 1789. And – again as in 1789 – extremism on the one hand called forth extremism on the other. The autocratic, centralised nature of the State and the lack of industrial development (and thus of any concomitant bourgeois class) meant that the revolutionary movement in Russia tended to be composed exclusively of a rootless *intelligentsia* (the very word is Russian) who relied more on moral fervour, rhetoric and violence than on systematic, critical, detailed analysis.

Among the cacophony of dissenting voices on what should be done in Russia, the most radical was that formed by the Narodniks or Populists. As the name suggests, their most powerful attachment was to the people of Russia and the power of the ordinary peasant population to regenerate the nation. The Populists were eclectic in drawing on Western philosophy: Hegel, materialist trends, and various forms of socialism were all grist to their mill. Central to their concern was the defence of the Russian peasant commune, firstly against the capitalism so vigorously criticised by Western European socialists, and secondly as a basis for a socialist society in Russia. When it came to tactics, there were two schools of Populist thought: those who believed in the self-emancipation of the people and tried to achieve this by peaceful propaganda, and those who believed in the necessity of attacking the autocracy directly through small groups of terrorists. When the movement to propagandise among the peasantry in the mid-1870s had failed, a more close-knit organisation – *Zemlya y Volya* (Land and Liberty) – was formed but soon split into those favouring agrarian reform, who called themselves *Chernyi Peredel* (General Redivision), and those who put the accent on terrorist activity – *Narodnaya Volya* (People's Will). The latter achieved one of its aims in the assassination of the Tsar in 1881 but found that this in itself accomplished nothing except the decimation of the group.

It was at this point that Marx's ideas began to have an impact on Russia. Indeed, Russian was the first language into which *Capital* had been translated: the official censor had passed it on the grounds that it was a 'difficult and hardly comprehensible' work that 'few would read and still fewer understand'. But Marx appeared to predict socialist revolution in the *West*: history moved through certain stages and communism could only follow when capitalism had already provided the industrialisation and working class to make it possible. This point was put with force by the Populists who claimed that their Marxist opponents could not be proper revolutionaries because, on Marx's view, they had to sit back and wait for capitalism to develop first, whereas, to quote Zhelyabov, the Tsar's assassin, 'History moves too slowly – it needs a push'. This argument was put to Marx himself in 1881 by Vera Zasulich herself a living legend for having shot General Trepov, Governor of St Petersburg, and been acquitted by the jury. Was Russia really unfit for socialism, she wanted to know, or was it possible, as some claimed, to bypass capitalism and start from the common ownership of land traditional in the Russian village? Marx's answer to this *cri de coeur* was positively sibylline:

The analysis given in *Capital* assigns no reasons for or against the vitality of the rural community, but the special research into this subject which I conducted, the materials for which I obtained from original sources, has convinced me that this community is the mainspring of Russia's social regeneration, but in order that it might function as such one would first have to eliminate the deleterious influences which assail it from every quarter and then to ensure conditions normal to spontaneous development.

However, the last two decades of the nineteenth century foreclosed that option for ever. For Russia had been experiencing its industrial revolution. The production of coal, steel and oil had increased many times over. But these were nevertheless differences from the West that were to prove significant later. Industrial development was very concentrated, with Moscow and St Petersburg as the only really large industrial cities. This meant that the working class, though small, was also concentrated. The development of Russian industry had been financed mainly from abroad and the state had played a large part, dominating the railways, the banks, and the timber trade. Thus there were proportionately fewer capitalists and no vigorous middle class.

Thus Lenin could declare by the end of the 1890s that the problem posed by the Populists had been overtaken by events: Russia was *already* capitalist. In his first major work entitled *The Development of Capitalism in Russia*, Lenin produced a clearly documented study of the emergence of capitalism out of feudalism in Russia, filling out some of the details that Marx would no doubt have put in his unfinished Volume Three of *Capital*. The stage of usury capital and merchant capital outlined by Marx had already been superseded in some places by manufacturing capital – capital applied directly to the productive system – and the next stage of industrial capital was already on the horizon. From this detailed analysis Lenin concluded that the proletariat held a unique position in that they were the only class fully to appreciate and be able to articulate the exploitation of all Russian labourers – including the artisans and rural proletariat. With the factory proletariat,

> exploitation is fully developed and emerges in its pure form, without any confusing details. The worker cannot fail to see that he is oppressed by capital, that his struggle has to be waged against the bourgeois class . . . That is why the factory worker is none other than the foremost representative of the entire exploited population.

This perspective – with its idea of the proletariat leading the population in the revolutionary struggle – governed Lenin's political thinking up to 1914. To many it has seemed that in Marx there is a lot of theory and little practical politics, and that in Lenin the reverse is true: Lenin is seen as the supreme tactician, the revolutionary opportunist, the seizer of chances. Trotsky put it in this way:

> The whole of Marx appears in the *Communist Manifesto*, in the *Critique of Political Economy*, in *Capital*. Even if he had never been destined to become the founder of the First International, he would still remain for all times the figure which we know today. The whole of Lenin on the other hand appears in revolutionary action. His scientific works are only a preliminary for activity. Even if he had never published a single book, he would live on in history, in the shape in which he has entered it, as the leader of the proletarian revolution.

But this gives a wrong impression. Lenin was indeed a supreme tactician but his practical politics, his 'line', was invariably based on a close theoretical analysis of the facts as he saw them. His idea of the Party was no exception. But the facts were Russian facts and, although the success of Lenin gave the Leninist Party world-wide currency, his Party was a distinctly Russian phenomenon.

Lenin's real name was not Lenin at all. Most leading revolutionaries had party names that they used to conceal their identity from the police – Lev Davidovitch Bronstein took the name Trotsky from one of his jailers and Joseph Vissarionovitch Djugashvili adopted Stalin – man of steel – for its obvious connotations of toughness. Lenin was born Vladimir Ilyich Ulyanov on 10 April 1870 in Simbirsk, a provincial capital several hundred miles east of Moscow. The city lay on the river Volga which, significantly, formed

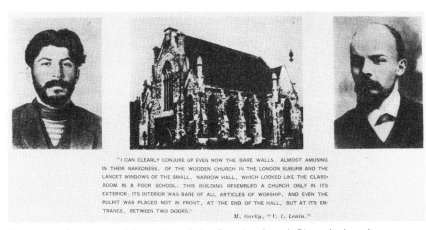

"I CAN CLEARLY CONJURE UP EVEN NOW THE BARE WALLS, ALMOST AMUSING IN THEIR NAKEDNESS, OF THE WOODEN CHURCH IN THE LONDON SUBURB AND THE LANCET WINDOWS OF THE SMALL, NARROW HALL, WHICH LOOKED LIKE THE CLASS-ROOM IN A POOR SCHOOL. THIS BUILDING RESEMBLED A CHURCH ONLY IN ITS EXTERIOR; ITS INTERIOR WAS BARE OF ALL ARTICLES OF WORSHIP, AND EVEN THE PULPIT WAS PLACED NOT IN FRONT, AT THE END OF THE HALL, BUT AT ITS EN-TRANCE, BETWEEN TWO DOORS."
M. Gorky, "V. I. Lenin."

Stalin and Lenin on either side of the Brotherhood Church, London, where the Fifth Congress of the Russian Social Democratic Labour Party met in 1907

the effective boundary between Europe and Asia: Lenin drew his political inspiration from both sides. Like Marx, he came from a family which was middle class, comfortably off and intellectual. His father was a school inspector who eventually became a nobleman, his mother a doctor's daughter and half German. When Lenin was sixteen, his idealistic elder brother Alexander was hanged for participating in a conspiracy to assassinate the Tsar. A year later Lenin went to the University of Kazan but got expelled in his first term for joining a protest against the university inspector. He nevertheless continued his studies, living with his family, reading widely and learning German in order to be able to read *Capital* and other works in the original. By the time he was allowed to go to St Petersburg in 1893 Lenin was already a committed Marxist. He had also perfected a passion for work. As a boy he had given up skating when it interfered with his studies. He periodically gave up chess, too, on the same ground. And the same was true of music. As he wrote later to Gorky:

> I can't listen to music too often. It affects your nerves, makes you want to say stupid, nice things, and stroke the heads of people who could create such beauty while living in this vile hell. And now you mustn't stroke anyone's head – you might get your hand bitten off. You have to hit them on the head, without any mercy, although our ideal is not to use force against anyone.

Lenin was nothing if not single-minded and self-disciplined.

A severe bout of pneumonia secured him permission to go abroad. He went to Paris where he visited Marx's son-in-law Longuet and then to Switzerland where he met Vera Zasulich and Plekhanov, then Russia's leading Marxist intellectual with whom Lenin declared himself to be 'infatuated'. Plekhanov, for his part, recognised the organisational genius that the movement needed. Lenin returned to St Petersburg to galvanise the underground movement but was promptly arrested and sent to Siberia for three years. However, life in Siberia did at least give him unlimited time for study: Tsarist penalties were generally much more lenient than those suffered later in Stalinist jails. Lenin translated *The Theory and Practice of English Trade Unions* by Sidney and Beatrice Webb. He also got married to Nadezhda Krupskaya whom he had met five years earlier in St Petersburg and who was to remain his lifelong companion. By the time Lenin returned from exile he had finished his major work on *The Development of Capitalism in Russia* which was actually published while he was still in Siberia. It was now time to turn his attention to the founding of a Party that would be instrumental in leading 'capitalist' Russia towards a socialist revolution.

As a first step, Lenin joined Plekhanov and fellow-exiles in Switzerland

Lenin playing chess in 1908 with a fellow-Bolshevik at the villa of Maxim Gorky on the island of Capri

to found a newspaper – the famous *Iskra* – which would not only establish a uniform policy line but, through its distribution network, create the Party organisation that had so long been lacking. Lenin set out his ideas on how this Party should be organised in his classic book *What is to be Done?* – the very title of which conveys his sense of driving practical urgency. It was to become the basic text on which all future Communist Parties were constructed. First of all, Lenin attacked those groups in Russia who organised campaigns inside the factories for better wages and working conditions. These groups came to be known as 'Economists' from their concentration on economic as opposed to political questions. According to Lenin, the Economists showed inadequate leadership and were unable to express the role of the proletariat as leader of all classes in the struggle against the autocracy. Basing himself on his own conclusions in *The Development of Capitalism in Russia*, Lenin declared that the Economists could not produce the initial organisation of the Party necessary to parallel politically the economic transition from scattered handicraft production to national capitalism. Since capitalism was organised on a national scale, the working class should be organised nationally, too, and not waste its energies in isolated and local efforts.

Lenin then elaborated his ideas on 'Social Democratic consciousness' by which he meant a proper Marxist assessment of the situation. (In those far-off days the words 'Social Democratic' and 'Marxist' were interchangeable.) This involved an intensive knowledge of the socio-economic situation and prospects of every class. It was therefore impossible for the proletariat, whose 'economic' struggle was too narrow, to achieve this consciousness. Lenin maintained that the proletariat, left to itself, would inevitably follow bourgeois ideology and continued in the key passage:

> Since there can be no talk of independent ideology formulated by the working masses themselves in the process of their movement, the only choice is – either bourgeois or socialist ideology. There is no middle course (for mankind has not created a 'third' ideology, and, moreover, in a society torn by class antagonisms there can never be a non-class or an above-class ideology). Hence, to belittle the socialist ideology in any way, to turn aside from it in the slightest degree means to strengthen bourgeois ideology. There is much talk of spontaneity. But the spontaneous development of the working-class movement leads to its subordination to bourgeois ideology; for the spontaneous working-class movement is trade-unionism, and trade-unionism means the ideological enslavement of the workers by the bourgeoisie. Hence, our task, the task of Social-Democracy, is to combat spontaneity, to divert the working-class movement from this spontaneous, trade unionist striving to come under the wing of the bourgeoisie, and to bring it under the wing of revolutionary Social-Democracy.

This view of the inadequacies of the working class if left to its own devices entailed positive proposals. Given the Party's task of assuming the role of leading all exploited classes in the democratic revolution, it must have an all-Russian organisation. This was best centred on an all-Russian newspaper such as *Iskra* aspired to be. Such an organisation could maintain contacts and doctrinal cohesion on an all-Russian basis, ensure specialisation and non-duplication, and maintain the leading position of the proletariat. Such an organisation would also have the attributes of secrecy, centralisation, specialisation, and exclusivity. But all these attributes would be dependent on Lenin's fundamental idea, which was the real point at issue in the later Bolshevik-Menshevik split: that the organisation should be composed of professional revolutionaries. They would be professional in two senses: they would devote themselves full time to party work and they would be fully trained: 'the struggle against the political police requires special qualities; it requires professional revolutionaries'. Their training would be based on scientific knowledge, itself a product of the bourgeoisie: 'The contemporary socialist movement can come into being only on the basis of a profound scientific knowledge . . . the bearer of this science is not the proletariat, but the bourgeois intelligentsia; contemporary socialism was born in the heads of individuals of this class'. Lenin was not against mass organisations – on the contrary – but he insisted that they must be quite separate from the party élite. Nor was Lenin against inner-party democracy, but this implied full publicity and election to all offices, and only an 'incorrigible utopian' could advocate this under present conditions in Russia. The leadership would therefore have to be chosen through the oligarchical principle of co-option. Lenin did have the grace to say later that his book 'should not be treated apart from its connection with the concrete historical situation of a definite, and now long past, period in the development of our Party.' The Economists, he said, had bent the stick in one direction: to straighten matters out, he had bent it in another. But matters stayed bent and the book was canonised, for obvious reasons, by Stalin.

The next task was actually to found the Party that Lenin had so forcefully described. The Congress that was summoned to achieve this finally met in a flour warehouse in Brussels in July 1903. Lenin was never a man to leave anything to chance if it could be planned in advance and he spent great time and energy in getting delegates chosen to the Congress who would reflect his own views. One of his colleagues at the time remarked: 'There is no other man who is absorbed by the revolution twenty-four hours a day, who has no thoughts other than of revolution, and who, even when he sleeps, dreams of nothing but the revolution.' All the same, the omens for creating a single, united All-Russian Social-Democratic Labour Party were not good: the forty or so delegates were noisy and argumentative people much given to backroom manoeuvring and factional intrigue. After twelve days in Brussels spent drafting a Party programme, the delegates were expelled by the Belgian police. They continued their excited discussions on the train and cross-channel ferry and went at it hammer and tongs for another twelve days in London.

In fact, the Congress which had assembled to found a new single Party ended up by creating two. It had begun well for Lenin with an almost unanimous condemnation of the Economists and a rejection of the federalist principle suggested by the delegates from the Jewish Trade Unions who wished to preserve a separate identity within the Party. But with the debate on the Party's rules this unanimity disappeared. Lenin's draft of Article

One read that a Party member was one who 'accepts the Party's programme and supports the Party both financially and by personal participation in one of its organisations'. But a slightly different version was proposed by Martov. Bohemian, gregarious, intensely intellectual and universally popular, Martov had been Lenin's closest friend and collaborator for several years. He preferred to say that a member 'accepts the Party's programme and supports the Party both financially and by regular work under the control and direction of one of the Party organisations'.

The difference might seem small but was absolutely vital. Lenin wanted a close-knit group of professional revolutionaries organised in a strict hierarchy: Martov advocated a much more European type of Party with a looser grouping of revolutionaries shading off through active amateurs into a mass movement. Martov's draft obtained a small majority but soon the Jewish delegates and the Economists walked out of the Congress, leaving Lenin's followers in the majority – Bolsheviks as opposed to the followers of Martov who came to be known as 'Minoritarians' or Mensheviks. The Bolshevik Party was born.

Yet the Congress was in many ways a pyrrhic victory for Lenin. He had used his majority to push through the strictest form of centralisation. His view (which he was admittedly sometimes later to modify) was that 'the organisational principle of revolutionary social democracy strives to go from the top downwards, and defend the enlargement of the rights and plenary powers of the central body against the parts'. The Congress and its aftermath illustrated Lenin's fundamental strength which was to stand him in such good stead in 1914 and 1917: his utter intransigence on basic principles and his consequent ability to stand alone against the world. Lenin relates the following conversation with one of the more moderate delegates to the London Congress. It is all the more interesting as Krupskaya (who should have known) tells us that it 'sums up Ilyich to a "t"':

'What a depressing atmosphere . . .' he complained to me. 'All this fierce fighting, this agitation one against the other, these sharp polemics, this uncomradely attitude!'

'What a fine thing our Congress is,' I replied to him. 'Opportunity for open fighting. Opinions expressed. Tendencies revealed. Groups defined. Hands raised. A decision taken. A stage passed through. Forward! That's what I like! That's life! It is something different from the endless wearying intellectual discussions which finish, not because people have solved the problem, but simply because they have got tired of talking.' The comrade of the 'Centre' looked on me as though perplexed and shrugged his shoulders. We had spoken different languages.

But Lenin was not without his critics, the most virulent of whom, Trotsky, was to be, with Lenin, the chief architect of the 1917 revolution. Trotsky was nine years younger than Lenin and his father was a relatively prosperous farmer, a *kulak*. The young Trotsky early turned to revolutionary activity, was arrested and, after more than four years of prison and exile, escaped from Siberia to the West. He eventually knocked at Lenin's door in London's King's Cross shortly before dawn on an October day in 1902. With the superb arrogance that characterised him all his life, he made it clear that Lenin would have to pay off the cabbie. Trotsky had a powerful literary style and was immediately welcomed onto the *Iskra* team. At the London Congress he was a staunch supporter of Lenin, even declaring that the Party's statutes should express 'the leadership's organised distrust' of its members who should be subject to vigilant control from above. His leader's subsequent ruthlessness, however, led Trotsky to revise his view of Lenin: he saw him as an imitation Robespierre bent on setting up a pseudo-Jacobin dictatorship over the masses, accepting or debarring local organisations on the simple principle of the seventeenth-century thinker Descartes 'I am confirmed by the Central Committee, therefore I am'. It was in this context that Trotsky made his famous prediction that Lenin's methods would lead to the following result: 'the Party organisation substitutes itself for the Party, the central committee substitutes itself for the organisation, and finally, a "dictator" substitutes himself for the central committee.' Although he came to forget his words in the extraordinary events of the 1917 revolution, Trotsky must often have bitterly remembered them in his later forlorn battle with Stalin.

The strident divisions of the Russian Marxists were soon overtaken by events. While the disputes were raging in London, Russia was experiencing the first general strike in her history. Matters came to a head on 'Bloody Sunday' – 9 January 1905 – when several hundred people were killed when troops opened fire on a peaceful demonstration assembled in front of the Winter Palace to present a petition. The image of the Tsar as 'the little father of his people' was shattered for ever. Army morale was lowered by a crushing defeat in the war against Japan. The situation deteriorated as the year wore on until the Tsar felt obliged in October to grant a constitution promising freedom of speech and a parliament. The following month saw the creation in St Petersburg of a Council – or Soviet – of Workers' Deputies to organise an intensified strike. The Mensheviks were the most active party in the creation of the Soviet: the Bolsheviks actually boycotted it at its beginning. In fact, the events of 1905 – more a series of profound anarchic disturbances than a revolution – had caught the organised revolutionaries by surprise and they only began to return to Russia in the late summer. The

January 1905: troops firing on workers in St Petersburg. 1905 saw a revolutionary movement in Russia which almost toppled the Tsar

Soviet was well under way before Lenin arrived. Only Trotsky had been in St Petersburg from the beginning. The Soviet gave him full scope for his talents as orator and organiser and, at twenty six, he was its dominant personality. But the success of the Soviet was short-lived. The strikes petered out and the military force which had sparked off unrest at the beginning of the year was able to quell it by the end.

1905 brought about a temporary unity among the Marxists and gave rise to the principle of 'democratic centralism' which has remained the classic, if highly ambiguous, description of Communist Party organisation ever since. Lenin declared the principles of *What is to be Done?* to be no longer applicable. The task now was 'to see to it that all higher-standing bodies are elected, accountable, and subject to recall. We must work hard to build up an organisation that will include all conscious Social-Democratic workers, and will live its own independent political life. The autonomy of every Party organisation, which hitherto has been largely a dead letter, must become a reality.' This optimism, however, declined as soon as the tide of reaction swept back in Russia: the Bolshevik party dwindled in numbers and was soon reduced to arranging marriages with wealthy heiresses and holding up banks to support its scanty resources. In any case, democratic centralism has been more often centralist than democratic. Indeed, the chief lesson that Lenin drew from 1905 was that victory would only be the consequence of a separate party strictly united on an agreed programme. Success was not to be found in any sort of wishy-washy compromise.

But what kind of a revolution should be aimed at? From their defeat in 1905, the Mensheviks drew the conclusion that socialism could only triumph by means of initial reforms gained by alliance with the liberals; their aims should therefore be restricted to the establishment of a democratic republic along West European lines. At the other extreme Trotsky (and he proved to be the more accurate forecaster) elaborated what was to become known as the theory of permanent revolution. For him, the working class had a significance in Russia that was out of proportion to its size in that the workers in large-scale industry were more concentrated and united than workers in smaller enterprises – and Russian industry was nothing if not large scale. And this industry was more exposed than in the West as it was not supported by a long-standing and all-pervasive capitalist ethic. The working class was in a position to paralyse industry and control urban centres as in few other countries. Trotsky asserted, therefore, that 'it is possible for the workers to come to power in an economically backward country sooner than in an advanced country'. But any proletarian government would soon find that it had to adopt increasingly socialist measures in order to retain its power. Any half-hearted measures would dispirit its own supporters and allow counter-revolutionaries to re-emerge. In other words, the bourgeois and socialist revolutions would have to be telescoped into a single process. The revolution would have to be permanent in another sense, too, in that it could not be confined to Russia. Successful revolution in the West would be a necessary condition for its survival. In between these two extremes lay the views of Lenin. He drew the opposite conclusions from the Mensheviks about the failures of 1905 – the liberals were totally unreliable allies in any revolutionary struggle. This led him to view the peasantry more optimistically and he can claim to be the first Marxist who proposed sharing political power with the peasantry. Hence Lenin adopted the curiously hybrid notion that Russia could have a revolution that would be bourgeois in its social and economic form (in that it would promote private enterprise and capitalist development) while being socialist in its political form (in that it would be spearheaded by representatives of the working class). It was only in the upheaval of 1917 that Lenin came to see that it was Trotsky who had been right all along.

What changed Lenin's perspective was the outbreak of war in 1914. War has frequently been the harbinger of revolution and Russia was to prove no exception. The war also produced an irredeemable split in the world Marxist movement whose cornerstone had always been its internationalism. The distinction between socialists and Communists really dates from August 1914. The workers, so the *Communist Manifesto* said, have no fatherland. But they did in 1914 – and even more so their leaders. The mighty German Social Democratic Party, hitherto in implacable opposition, voted their government war credits. In France, Jules Guesde, veteran revolutionary and collaborator of Marx himself, actually joined the cabinet as War Minister. At first, Lenin refused to believe the news but he quickly adjusted to the situation. The tiny Bolshevik party were the only Marxist group to see the war in a positive light. They became 'revolutionary defeatists' and adopted the slogan 'Turn the imperialistic war into civil war'.

As the war dragged on, Lenin devoted considerable attention to international affairs which previously had little occupied him. Particularly, following the English economist Hobson and the Austrian Marxist Hilferding, Lenin sought the key to the international situation in the phenomenon of imperialism. According to Lenin imperialism was tied to a change in the nature of capitalism – the growth of monopoly capitalism. This form of capitalism, he thought, had superseded competitive capitalism at the beginning of the twentieth century when the advanced economies came to be dominated by finance capital, controlled by banks which were themselves concentrated in cartels or trusts. The former type of capitalism was typified by the export of goods: monopoly capitalism exported capital. The surplus capital could not be used at home (for this would mean a decline in profits for the capitalists) but 'for the purpose of increasing profits by exporting capital abroad to the backward countries. In these backward countries profits are usually high, for capital is scarce, the price of land is relatively low, wages are low, raw materials are cheap.' This in turn led to the *de facto* division of the world into the various spheres of influence of international cartels. This analysis explained many things to Lenin. It explained the lack of serious economic crises from the 1870s onwards when Marx's dreaded law of the falling rate of profit seemed to have been overcome. It explained the 'betrayal' of the Marxist leaders in the West, for the super-profits of imperialism had made it possible to bribe the upper strata of the proletariat and corrupt the revolutionary fervour of their leaders. (Lenin did not go into the question of how many workers had been bought off or why the whole proletariat of the relevant countries should not be affected, or what effect this would have on revolutionary possibilities.) Finally, it explained the war. The productive forces of the younger and more energetic economies of Germany and Japan now needed to export capital and secure appropriate sources of raw material. For this they had to upset the established division of spheres of colonial influence. The 'uneven development' of capitalism, as Lenin called it, created problems that could only be solved by force.

In his Zurich isolation Lenin had begun to think that the imperialist war had brought world capitalism to its final stage and introduced the precondition for worldwide socialist revolution. Nevertheless, six weeks before the revolution, at the age of forty-six, Lenin told an audience of young Swiss workers that 'we of the older generation may not live to see the decisive battles of this coming revolution'. But when he heard that the Tsar had abdicated and a provisional Government had been formed, he made speedy preparations for his return: he was determined not to be late this time. He contemplated travelling through Germany disguised as a mute Swede but was persuaded to reject the idea as impracticable. Eventually the German government decided that the presence of Lenin in Russia was one of the best ways to secure Russia's withdrawal from the war and allowed Lenin and his followers secret free passage across Germany in the notorious sealed train.

Lenin eventually arrived in Petrograd (the Russified name for St Petersburg patriotically adopted at the beginning of the war) via Sweden and Finland on 16 April 1917. There he found a political situation that was inherently unstable. Now that the Tsar was gone, the Provisional Government headed by Kerensky, a provincial lawyer, was liberal in tone and had determined to summon an Assembly for the autumn to decide upon a constitution. But the government, with no policy except muddling through, only controlled the ramshackle bureaucracy and the increasingly disaffected army: their power was already being challenged by the resurrected Petrograd Soviet which was soon duplicated in other major towns. The Soviet could rely on the more immediate support of the general urban population, the factory workers and the radically-minded sailors in the nearby naval base at Kronstadt.

Until the arrival of Lenin, the Bolsheviks had vacillated and tended to align themselves with the Mensheviks in giving conditional support to the Provisional Government – which is not surprising in that, as orthodox Marxists, they considered themselves to be in the middle of a *bourgeois* revolution. However, Lenin soon changed all that. He went straight from the Finland Station to the Bolshevik Headquarters in the Palace of Ksheshinskaya, a former ballet dancer much favoured by the Tsar. There he unequivocally denounced the policy pursued by the Bolshevik leaders – particularly Stalin and Kamenev, editors of the Party newspaper *Pravda*, who had advocated conditional support for the Government (and therefore the war) and co-operation with the non-Bolshevik majority in the Soviet. The effect of Lenin's speech was dramatic. One observer reported:

July 1917: troops break up a street demonstration against Kerensky's provisional government

I'll never forget the thunderous speech, startling not only to me, a heretic who accidentally dropped in, but also to the faithful – all of them. It seemed as if all the elements of universal destruction had risen from their lairs, knowing neither barriers nor doubts, personal difficulties nor personal considerations, to hover over the banquet chambers of Ksheshinskaya, above the heads of the bewitched disciples.

Lenin summed up his ideas in his famous *April Theses* which said that:

the specific feature of the present situation in Russia is that the country is passing from the first stage of the revolution – which, owing to the insufficient class-consciousness and organisation of the proletariat, placed power in the hands of the bourgeoisie – to its second stage, which must place power in the hands of the proletariat and the poorest sections of the peasants.

The party should therefore deny support to the Provisional Government, give up its idea of reuniting with the Mensheviks, and agitate among the masses for an end to war, nationalisation of all land, and 'all power to the Soviets'. Lenin had, in fact, stolen Trotsky's clothes. The changed situation created by the war brought Lenin to revise his previous criticism of Trotsky that 'whoever wants to approach socialism by any other path than that of political democracy will inevitably arrive at the most absurd and reactionary conclusions'. And Trotsky, in turn, revised his views on the Leninist principles of organisation and joined the Bolsheviks in the summer.

Lenin was nevertheless insistent on the need to have mass support in any overthrow of the provisional government. Any other course, any attempts to act in the name of a minority, would be 'senseless Blanquism'. But in July a series of massive demonstrations that the Bolsheviks had half-heartedly supported nevertheless led to the suppression of the Bolsheviks by the Provisional Government supported by the Mensheviks and Social Revolutionaries. Lenin's conclusion was that the Social Revolutionaries and Mensheviks were traitors and that the Bolsheviks should go it alone. They would have been unsuccessful had it not been for the attempted military intervention by the commander-in-chief General Kornilov who moved his Cossack divisions on Petrograd in order, as he put it, 'to hang the German supporters and spies, with Lenin at their head, and to disperse the Soviet of workers' and soldiers' deputies so that it will never reassemble'. Kornilov was dismissed by Kerensky and his troops simply dispersed. But the affair restored the political fortunes of the Bolsheviks as it curtailed the room for manoeuvre of the more moderate parties and made it appear that the only alternative to a dictatorship of the right was one of the left – which has been a continuous aim of Communist tactics ever since. Both the Petrograd Soviet with Trotsky as its president, and the Soviet of Moscow fell under Bolshevik influence. Unorganised revolt was widespread in the countryside. By mid-September Lenin – still in Finland – wrote to the Central Committee: 'The Bolsheviks, having obtained a majority in the Soviets of workers' and soldiers' deputies of both capitals, can and must take State power into their own hands.' Most of the Party leaders still in Russia, mindful of the July defeat, were loath to take Lenin's suggestion seriously. He had to go as far as threatening to resign from the Central Committee and appeal to the ordinary members in order to stir his colleagues to decisive action which he only finally managed to implement by coming to Petrograd in person in mid-October. Even so, such influential members as Zinoviev and Kamenev (and they were not alone) continued to oppose insurrection and even publicised the split (and thus Lenin's intentions) in print. But the plans for insurrection, meticulously prepared and supervised by Trotsky, had their own momentum and when the Provisional Government attempted to close certain Bolshevik papers on 24 October the Bolshevik seizure of power began, a seizure which, at least in its initial stages, must be one of the easiest and most bloodless in all history.

Was October 1917 a revolution of the minority or of the majority? Was it a *coup d'état* in the style of Blanqui or a mass popular uprising? Revolutions

Bolshevik supporters demonstrating in front of the Winter Palace in 1917

are always *made* by minorities; and whether they have the support of the majority is always difficult to tell as revolutionary crises are not conducive to the holding of genuine elections. The Bolsheviks certainly did not have majorities in the Second Congress of Soviets that met in November 1917 or in the Constituent Assembly of the next month. More seriously from their own point of view, they did not enjoy the confidence of the only organised expression of proletarian opinion, the trade unions. But the despair of the Russian people and the virtual abdication of all other parties meant that power was almost presented on a plate to the Bolsheviks as the only Party resolute and disciplined enough to seem capable of radical solutions. From a broader perspective, the events of 1917 present several ironies. Firstly, of course, there is the success of the revolution in a country where traditionally Marxists had least expected it. Secondly, Marxism is not noted for the importance it accords to the individual. Yet Communists and non-Communists are agreed on the unique contribution of Lenin's genius. 'The role of the personality', wrote Trotsky, 'arises here before us on a truly gigantic scale.' Thirdly, the Bolsheviks had set out to create the freest society in the world. Yet (as we shall be seeing in the next chapter) the ensuing Stalinist period combined dictatorship with bureaucracy in a regime where, contrary to basic Marxist principles, political power seemed

October 1917: the storming of the Winter Palace

to dominate economics. Finally, in spite of Lenin's bitter opposition to the Populists twenty years earlier, it was the agrarian programme of their successors, the Social Revolutionaries, that the Bolsheviks adopted in preference to their own. And it was the support of the soldiers and ex-soldiers, the majority of whom were the long-distrusted land-hungry peasants, which assured the Bolsheviks of victory.

But this victory brought the Bolsheviks immediate problems. The quick success of the October revolution had taken them by surprise and they had no clear idea of how to construct their post-revolutionary State or how to lay the foundations of a socialist economy in a country already exhausted by years of war. There was little in Marx to guide them. The Bolsheviks had relied on the supposedly international nature of the revolution and the consequent help from a victorious West European proletariat to overcome the problems created by their own backwardness.

At the time it looked as though Germany were on the brink of the revolution which might guarantee lasting success to the enterprise of the Russian Communists. In the months that followed October, there was a genuine revolutionary movement in the big munitions factories in Germany, the start of a national revolutionary movement. The German people were war-weary and short of food. The German navy was mutinous and Germany was defeated in the field by the Allies. And yet the German revolution miscarried. In Kiel, Wilhelmshaven, Hamburg, Cologne and Hanover, the north of Germany was in revolt, mutinous sailors and soldiers in command. The Bavarian socialists proclaimed a socialist republic. Much of this was spontaneous and incoherent, but at the centre of many of the uprisings were the forerunners of the German Communist Party known as the Spartacists after the leader of the revolt of the slaves in the Roman Republic. The Spartacists were few in number. They were led by Karl Liebknecht, whose father had been a close friend of Karl Marx and a founder of the German Socialist Party, and by Polish-born Rosa Luxemburg, the intellectual equal of Lenin, who had been the leading left-winger among the German socialists for two decades. Soon mass demonstrations signalled the imminent revolution. The Communists made an assault on and captured important buildings in the centre of Berlin. Then the Social Democrats, who had found power virtually thrust into their hands on the fall of the Kaiser, turned to the military. But it was hard to find regular troops who could be relied on, so they had to rely on the newly raised Free Corps. A few days later Free Corps troops attacked the Communist strongholds and captured them easily. They were heavily armed and the Communists were ill-prepared. Karl Liebknecht and Rosa Luxemburg were brutally murdered. Rosa's body was dumped into the Landwehrkanal where it lay for more than three months. These murders – done by the Free Corps at the request, or so it seemed, of the Social Democrats who governed the country – caused a deep wound in the Left in Germany. The Communists could not forget or forgive. Karl Liebknecht and Rosa Luxemburg and the manner of their death, cast a long shadow over Germany and all Western Europe, where shortly nearly every Social Democrat Party would split, with the revolutionary wing forming a separate Communist Party.

Meanwhile in the Soviet Union the Bolsheviks got little respite from the humiliating peace treaty that they signed with Germany at Brest-Litovsk in March 1918. Three months later, civil war broke out. The anti-Communist forces, known as the White Russians and considerably aided by Britain and France, came near to defeating the Bolsheviks in 1919. In order to survive, Lenin introduced the Draconian measures known as War Communism: large-scale nationalisation, forcible requisitioning of food supplies from the peasantry, and partial militarisation of the labour force under trade union officials appointed from above.

But War Communism could not last. By the time that the end of the civil war was in sight, it was clear that the emergency measures were exacerbating the country's economic problems rather than solving them. War Communism, according to Lenin, was 'in complete contradiction to all we had

A Bolshevik poster expressing their embattled self-image

previously written concerning the transition from capitalism to socialism'. On Lenin's initiative a New Economic Policy was adopted in 1921. The requisitioning system was replaced by a tax in kind which enabled the peasants to keep a fixed share of their surplus. This in turn led to the abolition of restrictions on free trade and the restoration of market relations between agriculture and industry. There was a certain amount of denationalisation, but only of small-scale enterprises, and industry was organised in trusts enjoying a limited market independence.

The state of siege mentality, the isolation of Russia on the world scene, the impression of one emergency after another had its disastrous effect on politics inside Russia. The first result was an increase in the domination of the Party which was enhanced by the suppression of opposition beginning with dissolution of the Constituent Assembly in January 1918. Before the revolution, Lenin had been in favour of the convocation of the Constituent Assembly, not apparently realising the inevitable clash with the slogan of 'all power to the Soviets'. The decision to dissolve the Constituent Assembly, for which the Bolsheviks had only obtained twenty-five per cent of the votes, was unavoidable for a Party that claimed to be pursuing the proletarian socialist revolution. For the largest party in the Constituent Assembly represented peasant interests and the whole structure of the Assembly was much more appropriate to a bourgeois democracy. The suddenness of the Bolsheviks' victory and the atmosphere of perpetual crisis meant that the Party, as the only coherent and disciplined body, almost inevitably took over the functions of government. There followed a growing equation of Party and State. It became difficult to distinguish between disloyalty to the Party and disloyalty to the State. The consequences of this are well described by E.H. Carr, the best historian of the Russian Revolution:

> On the one hand, loyalty to the state came to require acceptance of specific doctrinal conformities hitherto associated with the Party. On the other hand, dissent from Party doctrine or prescriptions incurred the moral stigma, and later the physical sanctions, hitherto reserved for disloyalty to the state . . . The mere existence of an efficient machinery of repression invited the use of it. Opposition became a crime because the means were now available to track it down and punish it.

The pressure of civil war and the tendency to equate anti-Bolshevism with the counter-revolution led to the eventual suppression of all opposition parties. The Social Revolutionaries, representing as they did the better-off peasantry, were basically hostile to the Bolshevik programme but this was not the case with the Mensheviks, whose popular support (despite the Bolshevik harassment) tended to grow. In June 1918 they were excluded from the Pan-Russian Congress of Soviets and systematically suppressed at the end of 1920.

The real turning point of the Russian revolution was the Tenth Congress of the Communist Party in March 1921. It met only weeks after the brutal suppression of a mutiny at the Kronstadt naval base, formerly one of the chief bastions of revolutionary enthusiasm. Previously, Lenin had insisted on the right of all tendencies within the Party to free expression and their proportional representation in the Party Congress. Now, on Lenin's own proposal, all factions inside the Party were banned. The increasingly monolithic nature of the Party made it easier for those in control to enforce their domination. In March 1919 a five-man Political Bureau (Politburo), which had had a brief existence before the seizure of power, had been reconstituted. The civil war had meant that many major decisions could only be taken by a few, and the Central Committee of twenty-seven members was too unwieldly. An Organisational Bureau and a Secretariat were established at the same time. Only Stalin was a member of all four bodies.

The rise of Stalin coincided with the decline of Trotsky. In May 1922, Lenin suffered a stroke which paralysed his right hand and leg and impaired his speech. With Lenin incapacitated, it was natural that the other Politburo members Stalin, Zinoviev and Kamenev should form a bloc to oppose Trotsky who was still the most prestigious of the Bolshevik leaders. Trotsky singularly failed to react to his threatened exclusion from power. In particular, he

Above: Lenin addressing troops about to depart for the civil war front in 1920. *Below*: In subsequent copies, Trotsky, standing to the right of the podium, has been painted out

An anti-Bolshevik poster issued during the civil war and showing
Trotsky and Lenin plotting world revolution

did not exploit Lenin's criticisms of Stalin. Although Lenin never completely recovered from his stroke (he died in January 1924), he did manage
to dictate a kind of Testament in which he referred to Trotsky's 'outstanding ability' and described him as 'personally perhaps the most capable man
in the present Central Committee'. Of Stalin, he said: 'Comrade Stalin,
having become Secretary General, has unlimited authority concentrated in
his hands, and I am not sure whether he will always be capable of using that
authority with sufficient caution.' (Lenin was not often given to such under-
statement). Moreover, Trotsky had failed to champion the cause of inner-
party democracy. But the waning of Trotsky's influence was determined by
larger factors than internal rivalries in the Politburo. With the civil war at an
end, the Commissariat of War was no longer at the centre of attention and
Trotsky's particular administrative élan no longer in demand. Alone of the
Politburo members Trotsky, a late recruit to Bolshevism, had no independent power base in a Party organisation. The possibilities of revolution in
Europe (to which Trotsky attached particular importance) were receding

Lenin and his wife Krupskaya in 1922

and the country in general – exhausted by the 'heroic' age of which Trotsky was a symbol – longed for a respite and a period of reconstruction.

In the vital area of economic policy, Trotsky was ill at ease with Stalin's novel idea of socialism in a separate country which pretended to develop in disregard for the world economy in general. But Trotsky's position was not only an economic one. Basing himself on the whole thrust of the Marxist tradition from the *Communist Manifesto* onwards, he did not abandon his view that socialism could only be achieved in Russia through world revolution. The building of socialism was in any case a very lengthy process and the view of Stalin and Bukharin seemed to him to prejudice the entire international orientation of the Party and to despair of the revolutionary potential of the world proletariat. But Stalin's perspective was more attractive to Party members. With the failure of revolution in Western Europe, there was a growing feeling that the European proletariat was not to be relied on and even a certain disdain for the inefficiency of European Communists as opposed to the victorious Bolsheviks. The country as a whole was exhausted by years of repulsing external aggression and of civil war and eager now for some policy of economic progress. Socialism in one country seemed to present a clear and optimistic framework in which to pursue economic goals. And there was also the temptation of harnessing nationalistic sentiments and a proud feeling of independence to further the pursuit of economic aims. Trotsky continued to defend his view eloquently at the Party Congresses but met only with hostility. He was hampered by his previous equation of right with might and his self-proclaimed view that 'in the last instance, the Party is always right'. He became increasingly isolated and, in spite of a last-minute attempt by Zinoviev and Kamenev to rally a United Opposition against Stalin in 1926, Trotsky was expelled from the Party in 1927, from Moscow in 1928, and from the Soviet Union in 1929. With Stalin firmly in power, the next decade would see the revolution devouring its children instead of just exiling them.

4

COMRADES AND CITIZENS

To try to oppose the Party to the people is like trying to oppose the heart to the human body.

Leonid Brezhnev

A man gets into a bus and pushes into other passengers, saying 'Excuse me, gentlemen'. The conductor corrects him: 'You shouldn't say "gentlemen", you should say "comrades".' 'Oh no', he replies, 'comrades don't take buses, they have big black cars'.

Old Communist Joke

To foreigners the most familiar Russian events are the big parades on May Day and on 7 November, the anniversary of the Bolshevik revolution. These occur in Moscow's vast Red Square flanked on three sides by the multi-coloured onion domes of St Basil's Cathedral, the GUM department store and the Lenin Mausoleum. The November parade is devoted to a display of military strength: tanks, rocket launchers, gigantic intercontinental missiles file past for hours on end. On May Day, the parade concentrates more on impeccable displays of gymnastics and dancing by thousands of well-drilled young people. What do these events indicate about Soviet society?

Firstly, there is a strong impression of order. Communism represents an established order which is already here. In the West, Marxism is a doctrine which is critical and subversive: it is, in its own view, the creed of the underdog. In the Soviet Union, Marxism – or rather Marxism-Leninism – serves to legitimate an already established social and political system. It is, therefore, an essentially conservative ideology. This sense of stability has increased in the last two decades under the domination of Brezhnev. After the terror and purges of Stalin and the unpredictable reforms of Krushchev, the continuity of the top echelons of leadership has been enhanced throughout the Brezhnev period with the result that the leadership has got older and older and the average age of the Politburo who gaze at the parade from atop Lenin's tomb is now sixty-six. Krushchev's rather wild proclamations of 'building communism' have given way to Brezhnev's sober slogan of 'developed socialism'. And there is every reason to suppose that this will continue under Andropov.

Secondly, despite the predictions of Marx and Lenin, it is clear that the state is very far from withering away. On the Soviet account, the state does not disappear (at least until the achievement of full communism) but takes on a new socialist form. For socialism is only a stage in the development towards communism and the state is necessary to protect socialist gains already made and ensure that the development towards communism continues. The state is also necessary to defend the interests of the Soviet Union against the hostility of the capitalist world.

The funeral ceremony of Leonid Brezhnev in Red Square. The Lenin Mausoleum is on the left and the walls of the Kremlin behind it

Thirdly, and most importantly, the Red Square parades indicate the power of the Party whose leaders preside over the whole elaborate ceremony. The Party is the supreme force in the Soviet Union. It was attempts to question the 'leading role' of the Communist Party that brought about the invasion of Czechoslovakia in 1968 and the introduction of martial law in Poland at the end of 1981. The present Communist Party in the Soviet Union is very different from that created by Lenin. The first generation of communists, Lenin's colleagues, were intellectuals of middle-class back-

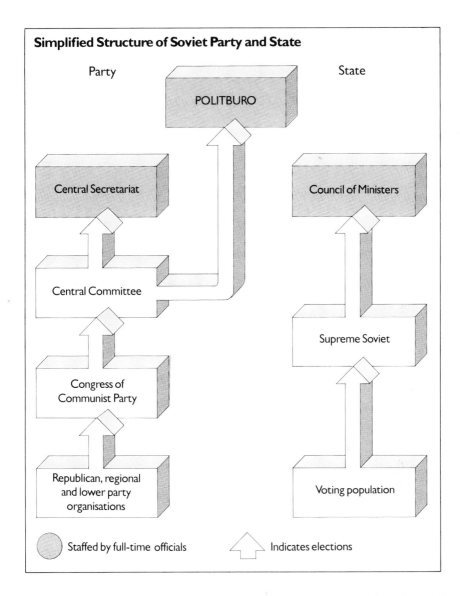

Simplified Structure of Soviet Party and State

Party   State

POLITBURO

Central Secretariat   Council of Ministers

Central Committee

Supreme Soviet

Congress of
Communist Party

Republican, regional
and lower party   Voting population
organisations

○ Staffed by full-time officials   ⬆ Indicates elections

ground who joined the Party when adult. The second generation, those of the 1930s and 1940s, were more men of peasant background who joined the Party early in life. They had little higher education and specialised in co-ercive political organisation. In the post–Stalin period, the Party has come to be dominated by men with a very high degree of technical education, specialists in administration and business management. The original generation of Marxist revolutionaries were highly individualist, people who had made personal and often dangerous commitments in order to create a new society. The present generation, by contrast, have themselves been created by this new society, born within the stable and all-enveloping embrace of the Party.

The control of the Party over all important areas of social life is immense. At the top of the Party is the Politburo with about a dozen full and eight candidate members who meet weekly. It is formally elected by the Central Committee which has 319 full and 151 candidate members who only meet twice a year and are elected by the Party Congress. The Central Committee has a vast secretariat with departments which deal with all aspects of political and social life and keep an eye on the general functioning of the Party which has about 200,000 full time workers or *apparatchiks*. It is control of the secretariat by the General Secretary which has made this the most powerful position in the Soviet Union from Stalin onwards. The power and influence of the Party is further enhanced by the system of *nomenklatura*. This is the list of positions either appointed directly by the Party or for which Party approval is necessary. Thus the *nomenklatura* of the Central Committee consists of cabinet ministers, important ambassadors, the Party secretariat etc. And the Party secretariat has its own *nomenklatura* and so on down the line extending to some three or four million jobs in all. The Party has an organised unit at every administrative level from republic and province down to village. There is a Party organisation in every school and in every factory.

The result is a vast system of patronage and a strong sense of hierarchy and secrecy. This was somewhat mitigated under the maverick Krushchev, who liked to be seen in public and, on one famous occasion, after being defeated in the Politburo actually appealed to the Central Committee – and won. There were no such upsets during the Brezhnev years. The leaders are screened from the rest of the population by special facilities which render them virtually invisible. And the Politburo certainly has no public relations office or press secretary. It is important to remember that membership of the Communist Party in the Soviet Union is not something that is open to all. In the West, political parties try to increase their membership by recruiting drives. But the seventeen million members of the Communist Party of the Soviet Union constitute a kind of élite and membership is a prize to be won, evidence of social and political success which opens all kinds of doors.

The current Soviet order is the creation of one individual more than any other – Joseph Stalin, man of steel. Although the revolution was dominated by Lenin, it was Stalin who shaped the society created by the revolution. He was born in backward Georgia and only spoke Russian as his second language. Son of a cobbler and one-time student at a religious seminary,

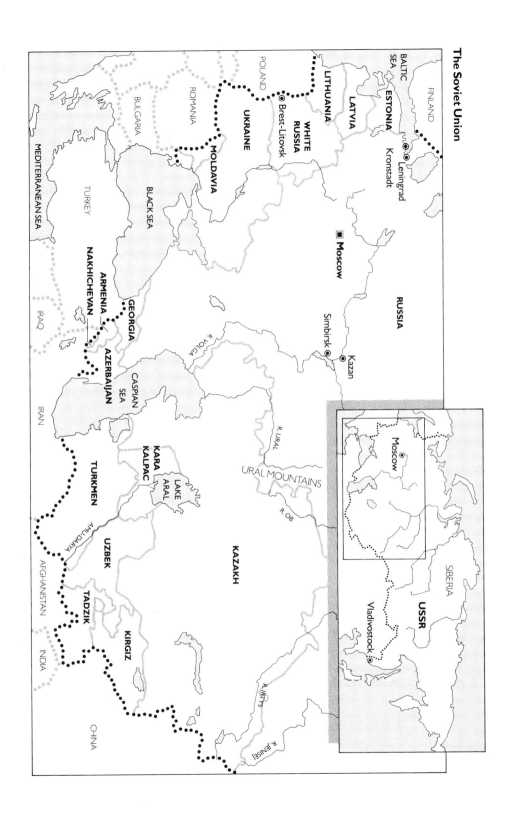

The Soviet Union

Stalin was neither an original thinker nor a great writer or speaker. He was essentially a cautious organiser, a loner who knew how to bide his time and how to play on the weaknesses of other people rather than draw out their strengths. Stalin's innovation was to subordinate everything (including the international dimensions of Bolshevism and the structure of the Party itself) to the goal of rapid heavy industrialisation at the expense of the agricultural sector. In the mid-1920s, Stalin had poured scorn on the 'super-industrial-isers' such as Trotsky, who suggested that Russia's output should be increased by almost twenty per cent per annum. But once he had decisively ousted Trotsky from all influence in the Party, Stalin in effect took over his policies. In the middle of 1929 capital investment was suddenly increased by as much as five times and the decision taken to go for mass collectivisation of agriculture. This mammoth effort could only be achieved by a united Party. The two years preceding were occupied by the last great debate in the Bolshevik Party between those who advocated a development of the Soviet economy based on the principles of the New Economic Policy (which tried to promote the spirit of private enterprise among the peasants) whose lead-ing spokesman was Bukharin, and those who put absolute priority on increasing industrial production, the newly-adopted policy of Stalin.

Bukharin defended what had become the New Economic Policy (and anti-Trotskyist) orthodoxy of progress through agricultural expansion on the United States model. Reluctantly in January 1928 he agreed to tempor-ary measures of a punitive sort to wrest their surpluses from the better-off peasants or *kulaks*. In the power struggle that followed, Bukharin and his followers were doomed from the start. In vain did he quote incessantly from Lenin's later articles on co-operatives and emphasise how vital Lenin con-sidered the preservation of the alliance with the peasantry. Bukharin was in reality opposed neither to collectivisation – only insisting that it was a long-term aim that presupposed a certain stock of machinery, etc. – nor to planned industrialisation – provided it was gradual and flexible. But the 'Right Opposition' – as Stalin cleverly managed to dub Bukharin and his followers – were hampered by the fact that the struggle was fought out in the top Party organs where Stalin was firmly entrenched. They had strong support among the rural masses and even urban workers, but were precluded from appealing to it by their previous condemnation of factionalism and the insistence on unity and conformity to Party decisions that they themselves had used with such effect against the Trotskyists two years earlier. Stalin's control of the Party machine was overwhelming and, indeed, the very nature of the Party had changed radically with a threefold increase of membership between 1924 and 1928. More generally, the 'Right' was associated with pessimism whereas Stalin right through until mid-1929

The Stalin terror: a resolution condemning those on trial for treason in 1938 is read out before cowed workers in a Moscow factory

could present himself as a man of the centre equipped with forceful solutions to the country's problems such as would appeal to the growing mass of pragmatic administrators. By July 1928 the 'Rightists' had failed to convince the Central Committee and lost their potential majority on the Politburo.

Now more than ever in control of the Party, Stalin radicalised his policies. Throughout 1928 the problem of grain supplies continued and, although in the summer of 1928 he still rejected the notions of class war in the country-side and expropriation of the *kulaks* (the first Five Year Plan provided for collectivisation of only twenty per cent of farming by 1933), a rapid change was evident during the last six months of 1929, presaging his 'revolution from above'. Decisions were increasingly taken by Stalin alone, relations with the peasantry worsened, the anti-Right campaign grew in violence, and there was a building-up of the 'cult of the personality' to counteract the obvious difficulties facing the government in its collectivisation campaign.

The gathering storm broke in December 1929. Stalin declared in a speech to the Marxist agrarians that the Party had 'recently passed from the policy of restricting the exploiting proclivities of the *kulaks* to the policy of eliminating the *kulaks* as a class'. He continued: 'It is ridiculous and fatuous to expatiate today on the expropriation of *kulaks*. You do not lament the loss of the hair of one who has been beheaded', and concluded, in a statement that spelt death for millions: 'there is another question which seems no less ridiculous: whether the *kulak* should be permitted to join the collective farms. Of course not, for he is a sworn enemy of the collective farm movement. It is clear, one would think'. From October 1929 to March 1930 the percentage of those in collective farms rose from four to fifty-eight per cent. The chaos and abuses were widespread and Stalin ordered a halt. By September 1930 the percentage had dropped to twenty-one. But by the end of

Stalin, the architect of the Soviet Union's rapid industrialisation, inspects new tractors in 1935

1930 it had risen again to more than fifty per cent and to seventy-five per cent by 1934. This enormous upheaval led to some ten million people being deported and bitter resistance by large sections of the peasantry which was not confined to the *kulaks* – itself a vague description which did not exceed four per cent of the peasantry. Party cadres were almost totally unprepared for the rapid change of policy. Famine was widespread and millions died as the government – now at last firmly in control of the agricultural sector – insisted on retaining, and even increasing, the grain procurements for the cities. Agricultural production took many years to recover to the levels of the late 1920s (over half the livestock had been slaughtered by the desperate peasantry) but foundations for the rapid industrial expansion of the 1930s had been firmly laid.

The economic upheavals of the 1930s represented (and still represent) a heroic age in the Soviet mind. Although Soviet agriculture has never recovered from its forced collectivisation, the development of heavy industry went on apace. Lenin had said: 'Communism is Soviet power plus electricity.' Huge hydro-electric projects were begun, canals dug and railways constructed. Industrial advances that it has taken Western nations several decades to achieve were telescoped into a few frantic years. The Soviet Union became a shining example for many of what socialism meant. There was a stream of foreign visitors – Bernard Shaw, Sidney and Beatrice Webb, H.G. Wells – one of whom said, 'I have seen the future and it works.' What they did not always see was *how* the future was often made to work – by forced labour.

The repercussions of Stalin's policies on the Party were equally drastic. The purges of the late 1930s can be seen as the political counterpart of Stalin's economic policy. Although the Party had been weakened by the expulsion of the Bukharinists, many Trotskyists were lured back in time to support Stalin's left turn. The assassination in late 1934 of Kirov who was head of the Leningrad Communist Party gave the signal for the beginning of the purges: Zinoviev and Kamenev were among the first to be tried and executed for political opposition. The great show trials, culminating with that of Bukharin in 1938, effectively obliterated the possibility of any alternative government. As Isaac Deutscher has succinctly put it:

> Among the men in the dock at the trials were all the members of Lenin's Politburo, except Stalin himself and Trotsky, who, however, though absent, was the chief defendant. Among them, moreover, were one ex-premier, several vice-premiers, two ex-chiefs of the Communist International, the chief of the trade unions (Tomsky, who committed suicide before the trial), the chief of the General Staff, the chief political Commissar of the Army, the Supreme Commanders of all important military districts, nearly all Soviet ambassadors in Europe and Asia, and, last but not least, the two chiefs of the political police.

The government personnel was renewed from top to bottom. Some three million died, only three per cent of the delegates to the 1934 Party Congress reappeared in 1939, and, of the Central Committee elected in 1934, seventy per cent were shot. A wave of new administrators filled the spaces left by the purges and, in spite of a new 'democratic' constitution in 1936, even the trappings of formal democracy were neglected: during the long years of Stalin's ascendancy there were only four Party Congresses and only three of the Comintern.

The Soviet Union in the time of Stalin has often been equated with contemporary Nazi Germany under the general rubric of 'totalitarianism'. This is to ignore the very different results of the two processes. In spite of the appalling waste, excesses, destruction and widespread suffering, the policies of Stalin did achieve a large measure of lasting social integration and economic development. Nazi totalitarianism, by contrast, did not transform

German society. It offered no coherent framework for social advance. Its ideological ragbag of racial extremism and international expansion procured only world war and unprecedented holocaust.

There have been many changes in the Soviet Union since the Stalin era. In particular, the standard of living has increased considerably and the systematic use of political terror had disappeared. But four figures that came to dominate Russian life under Stalin still remain.

The Bureaucrat

All countries have bureaucracies – and all bureaucracies are anonymous, immobile, self-interested and inefficient. But in the Soviet Union bureaucracy is the country's major problem and one which dates from the immediate aftermath of the revolution. Lenin had quickly to abandon his idea of workers' control in which the administration of people would give way to the administration of things. The growth of bureaucracy was encouraged by the increased nationalisation programme caused by confiscations and the war effort. There was also the influence of the traditional bureaucratic methods of Russian autocracy, and the desire to find work for the increasing number of unemployed by absorbing them into the state machine. By the end of 1920 this administrative machine had swollen to almost six million employees – a growth that was in inverse proportion to the productive capacity of the economy. Although Lenin was in favour of recruiting bourgeois technicians and specialists and indeed giving them special privileges, he was incessant in his conflict with bureaucracy. 'All of us', he wrote, 'are sunk in the rotten bureaucratic swamp of "departments".' Even the famous Rabkrin, designed in desperation to be a popular watchdog over the administration, became yet another body with all the deficiencies which it was supposed to combat. Lenin's remarks on the subject during the last months of his active life are akin to despair.

Under Stalin and his successors, the impact of the bureaucracy has increased enormously, particularly under the influence of the massive Five Year Plans. Of course, the plans have many things to their credit. They have made it possible for resources to be directed straight into building up the social services. Since the Plan eliminates the influence of consumer demand, it enables selective emphasis to be placed on producer goods such as hydroelectric plants, mines, railways and space platforms. The overall output of the Soviet economy has grown steadily and rapidly over the last fifty years. The economic cycle of expansion and recession so familiar in the West is minimised by the Plan. And the Soviet Union has surpassed the United States in the traditional indicators of industrial strength such as the output of steel, oil and cement.

Nevertheless, the Plan has severe disadvantages. Since the objectives of the Plan are couched in quantitative terms, the first casualty is quality. For example, the output of plate glass is measured in terms of square metres. So there is a tendency to increase production figures by making thinner glass. The result is that there are a lot of broken windows in Russia. Most individually produced goods are of such poor quality that they could not compete in Western markets. The productivity of the average Russian worker is much lower even than that achieved in 'inefficient' Britain. There are two reasons for this. Firstly, in any minutely planned economy small errors tend to have magnified repercussions (since everybody's output is somebody else's input). Secondly, the imposition of monthly (and quarterly and annual) quotas and deadlines leads to a frantic rush or 'storming', as the Russians call it, at the end of each month when the factory moves into a frenzied rhythm to fulfil that part of the Plan, a rhythm which has been impossible earlier in the month due to non-delivery of vital parts and exhaustion of workers from the previous 'storming'. There is also the problem that directors will camouflage hidden resources and keep them against a rainy day rather than overfulfil their objectives and have them raised as a consequence. Indeed, the main weakness of the Plan is that it discourages technical innovation which would only create problems for directors already locked into an existing supply system. The classic illustration of this is Vladimir Dudintsev's famous novel *Not By Bread Alone* where the hero, Lopatkin, is involved in an incredible struggle with the bureaucracy to get his invention of a machine for the centrifugal casting of iron drainpipes accepted. There were attempts under Krushchev to increase incentives and a form of profit in order to measure the relative efficiency of different enterprises. But this has not progressed very far and cannot – without fundamentally altering the Soviet system of economic and thus political control.

One major consequence of the Plan, evident to any visitor to Russia, is the existence of a widespread 'unofficial' economy. This is more than simply a black market. It is a permanent *doppelgänger* of the planned economy and an essential lubricant to the stiff strait-jacket of the system. This counter-economy probably accounts for over ten per cent of the Gross National Product. From private kindergarten places and priority medical treatment to domestic plumbing and heavy industrial materials, there is virtually nothing that cannot be obtained 'on the left' as the Russians (rather ironically) put it. The unofficial economy is particularly developed in the area of consumer goods which, in almost chronic short supply, are sold under the counter at a premium or bought up by speculators for profitable resale – or, indeed, both. There is also a 'grey' market in secondhand cars which seldom if ever exchange at the price fixed by the state. This freewheeling economic activity is most developed in the southern republic of Georgia where there thrives a distinctly Latin disregard for authority and the atmosphere is more reminiscent of the Mediterranean seaboard – Marseilles or Palermo – than of Moscow. In the early 1970s, one Otari Lazishvili was found to have become a millionaire through organising a network of illicit factories producing high quality clothing, the raw materials for which were all swindled from state enterprises. Lazishvili had enjoyed the protection of Mzhavanadze, First Secretary of the Georgian Communist Party and a member of the Politburo itself, who was himself dismissed.

The Ideologue

This figure is the counterpart in the realm of ideas to the bureaucrat in the economy. He is typified by Mikhail Suslov, grey guardian of the Party's ideological purity for twenty-five years. Before his death in 1982, he was held by many to be the person most responsible for Krushchev's fall. There is an inherent implausibility in the official Marxist-Leninist view that the Party always knows best; that the Party represents and is united with the people; and that the Soviet Union is a genuinely socialist state run for the benefit of the workers and triumphantly progressing along the road towards communism. Nevertheless, Marxist concepts do set the style for Soviet politics. Compulsory classes on Marxism-Leninism certainly lead to boredom and cynicism, but the general ideas do appear to be broadly accepted by a majority of the population. Of course, contradiction between ideology and reality is not confined to the Soviet Union: the United States of America, founded on principles of equality and liberty, were quite agreeable to incorporating States whose economies were based on slavery. But the role of ideology in the Soviet Union is all the more important as the Bolsheviks have no traditional legal right to rule. The legitimacy of the Communist Party depends directly on the validity of its ideology. The main newspapers of the Party – *Pravda* ('Truth') – and of the Government – *Izvestia* ('News') – are much occupied in strengthening the ideological front. According to an old joke, *Pravda* is not news, and *Izvestia* is not true. The pervading censorship sometimes has extreme consequences. The career of Lysenko, whose view that environment could alter hereditary characteristics, was enforced by Stalin and Krushchev as the only proper 'Marxist' biology, stifled Soviet studies into genetics for twenty-five years. Most notorious are the rewritings of history in which whole episodes (the Nazi-Soviet pact of 1939) or people (Trotsky) disappear without trace. There is a story concerning an entry in the *Great Soviet Encyclopaedia* on Beria, Stalin's police chief who was executed after being ousted by Krushchev. The editors of the *Encyclopaedia* were anxious to expunge the memory of Beria after his fall and pro-

The Paris Commune of May 1871. The barricade of the Place Blanche
defended by the women of Montmartre

Above: 'The Red Ploughman', a Soviet poster to encourage agriculture. The translation reads, 'On the wild field amid the ruins of evil Lordship and Capital, we shall drive our plough, and gather a good harvest of happiness for the whole working people.' *Opposite*: Anti-Bolshevik poster from the end of 1917. The translation reads, 'ORDER Everything for the Red Army: pitiless repressions, the most unjust seizures, confiscations, requisitions are allowed by the military commissar in the interests of the Red Army. Let children perish, let women die from hunger, let peasants be deprived of grain for sowing, let moaning and weeping be heard throughout the countryside – provided that the Red Army lacks for nothing.'

Big Boss Lev Trotsky

Note also the anti-Semitic portrayal of Trotsky

Above: Young Chinese women scan the Little Red Book below a portrait of Mao the Visionary. *Opposite:* The nursery of a People's Commune in China. The provision of crêches enables women to participate more fully in industry and agriculture

The two faces of modern Russia. *Top*: Despite persecution in the early years of the Soviet regime and more recently under Krushchev, the Orthodox Church is still a force in Russia. *Below*: A recent May Day parade in Moscow's Red Square

Fidel Castro addressing a mass meeting in Chile during the period when the Cuban Revolution was 'for export'

Cuba: Castro as Jesus in a modern painting above the entrance to Havana's municipal market

duced an article on the Bering Straits of exactly the requisite length which they then sent to owners of the *Encyclopaedia* with a request to paste it over the Beria original! But the most obvious result of ideological pressure is the sheer dearth of information in the Soviet Union. Statistics on social problems such as crime and alcoholism are officially unavailable. Natural disasters or aeroplane crashes usually go unreported. Information is rationed, a privilege only to be divulged to those with rank and influence. Even the death of Krushchev had to wait thirty-six hours to be reported – and then in a single paragraph.

The Policeman

Russia is not a police state today in the same sense that it was under Stalin. In the 1930s and 1940s the use of terror by the NKVD (as it was then called) was arbitrary and unpredictable. The number of political prisoners filling the labour camps ran literally into millions and the NKVD found itself in charge of a vast economic operation in which they were involved in providing a continuous supply of cheap labour, demand for which often determined the number of guilty. It is impossible to tell how many inhabitants there are today in Solzhenitsyn's Gulag Archipelago or prison camps. The Soviet Union does not provide figures. But most informed observers consider that the population is between one and two million of whom only a minute fraction are there for political reasons. Today, the KGB, current successor to the NKVD, does not intrude so much into the life of the ordinary Russian. Of course, every Soviet institution has its security section or First Department which keeps an eye on the political reliability of its members. Telephone tapping and censuring of letters is widespread. But more effective than direct political harassment are the various forms of economic pressure, particularly demotion or loss of job, that can be applied to those who oppose the system. This is the same tactic that was used against supposed dissidents in America during the McCarthy era; but it is far more effective in a society where the state has a virtual monopoly on employment and comments on social and political reliability form a regular part of an individual's dossier. Despite the provisions of the constitution, rights are difficult to enforce. The Marxist view of law in capitalist countries as the prop of the ruling class certainly applies to the Soviet Union: law is the prop of the new ruling class. The orginal revolutionary was a man of hope: the current citizen is a man who has learnt to walk carefully.

The Soldier

The sense of isolation and of being surrounded by hostile nations and hence the necessity of military preparedness is very strong in the Soviet

Union. The May Day parade serves to strengthen national morale and self-confidence. It is impossible to exaggerate the continuing impact of the Second World War in this context which is still an incessant theme of books, television programmes and films. The Great Patriotic War (as the Russians refer to it) is presented as the single-handed victory of the Soviet Union over Hitler. The result is that expenditure on defence and space exploration is given high priority and quality control is very strict: military production is separated from that of the rest of the economy in a manner unlike that of the West. Socially, however, the line separating military from civilian life is less clearly drawn than in the West. All schools and universities have some form of military training and there is two year compulsory National Service.

All this means that for many in the West, Marxism is largely a question of military threat. For Marxism is embodied in the Soviet Union and the Soviet Union, on this view, is bent on world domination. The Soviet military machine is geared up and ready to strike if ever the West were to lower its guard. The Soviet Union is the world's greatest military power on land. The Soviet Navy is second only to the navy of the United States. The Union of Soviet Socialist Republics spends a large share of her national income on armaments. Although comparisons are extremely difficult to make, the Americans claim that Russia spends more on arms than the United States. Over the years, Soviet tanks have overrun Eastern Europe. Soviet armed forces have subjugated nations that were once independent: Hungary, Czechoslovakia, Poland, the Baltic States. In East Germany a large and powerful Soviet tank army is poised to overrun Western Europe. A large Soviet army has occupied Afghanistan. Armies with Soviet military officers or instructors, Soviet backing and Soviet weapons have been active in Africa, the Middle East and Asia.

From the Soviet point of view, however, things look very different. Ever since the founding of the Soviet state in November 1917, the Kremlin has claimed to be employing force only for defence. And certainly, from the beginning, the Bolsheviks were obliged to defend the very long land frontiers they inherited from the Tsars of Imperial Russia. Those frontiers run for thousands of miles, from the Arctic, facing North Norway and Finland, across Eastern Europe to the Black Sea; then many hundreds of miles along the Turkish border, the frontier with Iran, and Afghanistan; then for thousands of miles with China. In the Far East, the Soviet Union faces Japan, and also the United States. Soon after the revolution, the Soviet frontiers were to be crossed by the invading armies of several allied nations: Britain, the United States, Japan, and several others. Invasion came from Poland, from Japan, and most terrible of all was the German invasion in 1941.

The devastation suffered by Stalingrad. The experience of the German
invasion left an indelible mark on the Soviet Union

By any standards, Russia's war losses were staggering. Some twenty million people died, seven million of them soldiers, the rest civilians, women and children. The siege of Leningrad lasted three years and nine hundred thousand of its citizens died. Most of European Russia was overrun by the German armies. Almost half of Soviet industry was destroyed. But in the Great Patriotic War, the Russians defeated the German armies and drove them back. Ever since, the Soviet leaders have claimed it was their country which did most to destroy fascism, and which suffered most. War has etched itself deep into the mind of every Soviet citizen. Every family has lost someone – a father, an aunt, a sister, a cousin.

So it is not surprising that today the Soviet Union has all the appearances of a garrison state and that the Soviet mentality is one of siege. It is, of course, also true that this attitude is fostered by Marxism-Leninism which sees the capitalist nations as the class enemy and necessarily hostile to its cause. Too great an accommodation with the West would undermine the legitimacy of the ideology. It would also weaken the internal position of the Soviet rulers who use tension with the West to justify restrictions on freedom.

In spite of the Communists' rhetoric about their inevitable victory and Communism being the wave of the future, it is difficult to see Soviet foreign policy as being anything but basically defensive. Even Soviet domination of

Eastern Europe is, in Soviet eyes, the creation of a buffer zone against the ever-feared resurgence of German militarism. Soviet suzerainty here was acquired with the full acquiescence of the Western powers. In a remarkable passage in his memoirs, Churchill records the rather nonchalant arrangement with Stalin:

The moment was apt for business, so I said, 'Let us settle about our affairs in the Balkans. Our armies are in Roumania and Bulgaria. We have interests, missions, and agents there. Don't let us get at cross purposes in small ways. So far as Britain and Russia are concerned, how would it do for you to have ninety per cent predominance in Roumania, for us to have ninety per cent say in Greece, and go fifty-fifty about Yugoslavia?' While this was being translated I wrote out on a half-sheet of paper:

Roumania	
Russia	90%
The others	10%
Greece	
Great Britain	90%
(in accord with USA)	
Russia	10%
Yugoslavia	50–50%
Hungary	50–50%
Bulgaria	
Russia	75%
The others	25%

I pushed this across to Stalin, who had by then heard the translation. There was a slight pause. Then he took up his blue pencil and made a large tick upon it, and passed it back to us. It was all settled in less time than it takes to set down . . . After this there was a long silence. The pencilled paper lay in the centre of the table. At length I said, 'Might it not be thought rather cynical if it seemed we had disposed of those issues, so fateful to millions of people, in such an offhand manner? Let us burn the paper.' 'No, you keep it', said Stalin.

The Soviet Union will go to almost any lengths to preserve its buffer zone: witness Hungary in 1956, Czechoslovakia in 1968 and Poland in 1981. But two factors are worth noting. Firstly, Soviet intervention generally has the support of the East European governments who fear for their own position if popular unrest in other countries should spread to their own. The 1968 invasion of Czechoslovakia, for instance, was an invasion by the Warsaw pact as a whole insisted on in particular by Ulbricht of East Germany and

Marshal Stalin looking very pleased with himself after the 1943 Tehran Conference with Roosevelt and Churchill

Gomulka of Poland. Secondly, in spite of the Brezhnev doctrine about maintaining 'Socialist solidarity', Russian aims in East Europe have little to do with Marxism. Mlynar, the only member of a Communist Politburo to have defected to the West, described Brezhnev's attitude at the tense meeting between Russian and Czech leaders in August 1968:

> Brezhnev spoke at length about the sacrifices of the Soviet Union in the Second World War . . . At such a cost, the Soviet Union had gained security and the guarantee of that security was the post-war division of Europe . . . It was all so simple, how could we fail to understand? Words like 'sovereignty' or 'national independence' did not come up in his speech at all, nor did any of the other clichés that officially justify the 'mutual interests of socialist countries'. There was one simple idea behind everything he said: during the war, our soldiers fought their way to the Elbe, and that is where our real Western borders are today. 'For us', Brezhnev went on 'the results of the Second World War are inviolable and we will defend them even at the cost of risking a new war.'

Russia's geo-political views spring from a naked expression of power that long predates Marxism.

The West has been misled by Communist rhetoric and consistently overestimated the quality of military resources available to the Soviet Union. The Sputnik of 1957 and Yuri Gagarin as the first man in space were indeed impressive achievements, but they were isolated events not supported by a comparable general scientific and technical development. During most of the post-war years the Soviet Union has been engaged, at tremendous cost, in an effort to catch up with American technology. In the last years of Stalin's rule, America developed the atomic and hydrogen bombs, enjoyed the world's most powerful economy, and, through its Nato allies, ringed the Soviet Union with missiles and bombers. It was not until the late 1960s that the Soviet Union developed the technology to deliver its own missiles. But it is the United States which, from the atomic bomb to the Cruise missile, has used its technological superiority to lead the way. Only in recent years has the Soviet Union been able to match its larger conventional forces with strategic weapons that are equal to those of America.

These four representative figures – the bureaucrat, the ideologue, the policeman and the soldier – were mainly the creation of Stalin. What would Lenin make of them, were he to arise from his tomb in Red Square? There are, of course, many aspects of what he would see that would sadden him. In his blueprint for Soviet society composed on the eve of the Bolshevik revolution, he wrote self-confidently:

Afghan rebels clamber aboard a Soviet armoured personnel carrier captured in April 1980

We ourselves, the workers, will organise large-scale production on the basis of what capitalism had already created, relying on our own experience as workers: we will reduce the role of the State officials to that of simply carrying out our instructions as responsible, revocable, modestly paid 'foremen and accountants'. Such a beginning on the basis of large-scale production will of itself lead to the gradual 'withering away' of all bureaucracy, to the gradual creation of an order without quotation marks, an order bearing no similarity to wage slavery, an order in which the functions of control and accounting – becoming more and more simple – will be formed by each in turn, will then become a habit, and will finally die out as the special functions of a special section of the population.

But things have not turned out quite like that.

The first thing that would surprise (and anger) Lenin is his own deification. The process began early: in the first year after his death, 6,296 items of Leniniana were published in the Soviet Union. He quickly became, as the official biography has it, 'the greatest genius of all time and all nations, master of all the treasures of human knowledge and human culture'. With Stalin rather an ambivalent figure and Krushchev virtually a non-person, the adulation of Lenin is perfectly safe. Lenin museums abound and ikons of Lenin are ubiquitous. Significantly, similar effigies of Marx are much harder to find. The growing monolithism of the Party, the political police in the form of the Chekha, and the problem of bureaucracy, were all evident in Lenin's lifetime and caused him considerable heart-searching. But the immense privilege of the Party and government élite, the colossal bureaucratic machinery of contemporary Soviety society, the rigidity of its ideology, and the imposition from above of the Five Year Plan were all unknown to him. As a constant critic of empty verbiage and social complacency, he would now have a lot of acid comments to pass.

Nevertheless, as a realist, Lenin would also be quick to appreciate the benefits of Soviet rule. The problem of illiteracy, for example, has been virtually wiped out: before the Revolution, only a quarter of the population were literate. As a result of the vastly-increased educational facilities, social mobility and equality of opportunity have been more firmly established in the Soviet Union than in most Western countries. Although an élite inevitably emerges and entrenches itself, it is based more on the possession of intellectual as opposed to material capital. The position of women (well over half the population owing to war losses) has also improved greatly. Immediately after the Revolution, divorce and abortion were made easier and women obtained at least formal equality in education and employment. Under Stalin the traditional family structure was reinforced by making divorce more difficult, penalising illegitimacy and prohibiting abortion. Stalin's measures have been largely repealed and, with equal pay for equal work and generous maternity care, women have greater equality in society at large than they do in the West. Within the home, however, women are still forced into an underprivileged status. The average Russian yields nothing in male chauvinism to his Western counterpart and most women have to bear the double burden of job and running a household. In the Communist Party, too, there are fewer women the further one rises up the hierarchy. Among the 250 or so members of the Central Committee there are only half-a-dozen women and none at all in the Politburo.

As befits a socialist state, the Soviet Union is proud of its social services. The range of pre-school provision is extensive, housing is cheap, and, above all, the provision of medical care, though of bad quality and full of shortages, is widespread and free. The Soviet Union trains more doctors than any other country and sends them to work where they are needed. In general, the grinding poverty and exploitation of pre-revolutionary times have been eliminated. And the twin evils of unemployment and inflation, so endemic in Western economies, are not objects of major concern to the Russians. Less tangibly, there is a strong feeling of the importance and depth of friendship. The sense of social solidarity and the importance of the collective is well developed. In Russian, there is no word for privacy.

Nevertheless, the Soviet Union is very far from being an equal society. What about 'We, the workers', in Lenin's ringing phrase? In spite of the original revolutionary ideals, Stalin was vehemently opposed to wage-levelling. Equality, he said, was a bourgeois concept. Instead, he was an ardent advocate of piecework and insisted that people should be rewarded in accordance with their productivity – a practice associated with the name of the coalminer Stakhanov, held up as an example to all Soviet workers in the 1930s. Consequently, despite considerable social mobility, the professional strata are tending to perpetuate themselves more and more. Income differentials are quite considerable: the ratio between the average income earned in industry and the highest is around 15:1. Although comparisons are notoriously difficult, it is fair to say that, in terms of earned income, there is more equality in the Soviet Union than in most Western countries. But it should be noted that actual money is nowhere near as important in the Soviet Union, as in the West. In an economy where the good things of life are in short supply and rigidly controlled, what matters most is access. Such things as a good flat, a new car, or even the best theatre tickets are not sold – they are allocated. This sort of inequality is at its starkest in the system of special shops reserved for the élite of Party and Government. These shops not only sell goods, often imported, that are never available to the general public, but their prices are also generally much lower than they would be outside. This arrangement amounts to a gigantic system of perks akin to those available in the more paternalist of American corporations. Those with access to this (carefully graduated) sort of privilege possibly number about one million. They constitute a ruling élite. Some have called them a ruling class. According to Soviet ideology, there are only two classes, workers and peasants, with an additional stratum of white collar workers and intelligentsia. However, in his famous book *The New Class*, the Yugoslav writer Milovan Djilas, defined ownership as 'nothing other than the right of profit or control' and argued that 'if one defines class benefits by this right, the Communist states have been, in the final analysis, the origin of a new form of ownership or of a new and exploiting class.' But the crucial difference from the class system in the West is that the Soviet rulers cannot pass on their material privileges in the form of inheritance and that the children of the élite have no privileged entry into the Communist Party hierarchy. It would be more accurate to characterise the Soviet Union as a 'rank' society where status and position on the social and political ladder are of overriding importance. At every level of Soviet society there is a pecking order of which all are aware. It is most evident, again, in the Red Square parades where the

The supply of consumer goods has risen steadily in the post-war Soviet Union: the GUM store in Red Square, Moscow

order of the leadership standing on the top of the Lenin mausoleum is very carefully calculated. Centuries ago Western envoys to the Kremlin would study pictures of the Tsarist court which reflected faithfully the exact rank and influence of the various officials. The art of Kremlinology still lives today.

One reason for the concentration of power and the emphasis on rank in the Soviet Union is the widespread belief there that strong government is necessary. As a nation, the Russians have an abiding fear of anarchy of which they have experienced, down the centuries, the worst sorts. They prefer to rely on strong government rather than on individual restraint in which they feel that their national character is all too lacking. The kind of national consensus achieved in countries such as America or Britain is the result of centuries of common national experience and social integration. The achievement of this consensus in the Soviet Union has been forcibly telescoped by the Party into fifty years. It is thought by many, therefore, to be young, fragile and in need of careful supervision. Moreover, Russia has had no experience of any government that has not been authoritarian, from Ivan the Terrible onwards. Peter the Great may have been responsible for opening up Russia to many Western ideas and practices: but he also first introduced organised censorship, political police, and the internal passport system that binds citizens to their domicile.

This historical background explains the lack of individuality in Russian public (as opposed to private) life. Government is something invisible and separate from the mass of the people who, therefore, do not feel in any way responsible for it or it for them. The whole individualist ethic intrinsic to Protestantism and Capitalism is entirely lacking in Russia. As a leading Russian dissident, Andrei Amalrik, wrote in his essay *Will the Soviet Union Survive until 1984?*:

> The idea of self-government, of equality before the law and of personal freedom – and the responsibility that goes with these – are almost completely incomprehensible to the Russian people. Even in the idea of pragmatic freedom, a Russian tends to see not so much the possibility of securing a good life for himself as the danger that some clever fellow will make good at his expense. To the majority of people the very word 'freedom' is synonymous with 'disorder' or the opportunity to indulge with impunity in some kind of anti-social or dangerous activity. As for respecting the rights of an individual as such, the idea simply arouses bewilderment. One can respect strength, authority, even intellect or education, but it is preposterous to the popular mind that the human personality should represent any kind of a value.

The mention of 1984 recalls George Orwell's allegory with its portrayal of totalitarian control, its Thought Police, and its Big Brother. But however fitting it may have been to many aspects of Stalin's régime, the nearer the Soviet Union has approached to 1984, the less appropriate is Orwell's picture. As already indicated, there is a fair amount of chaos and improvisation in the Soviet Union. And since the time of Stalin the political system has moved from a reliance on terror and the sheer force of ideology to persuasion based on material incentives. Moreover, there is no doubt that the mass of the people support the system. The Soviet state is two-thirds of a century old and few of its citizens are old enough to remember pre-revolutionary Russia. They have many grumblers but they are willing to put up with minor harassment, inefficient bureaucracy and stifling censorship in order to avoid the labour unrest, organised crime, political assassination and chronic unemployment which they perceive, however distortedly, as characteristic of the West. In this perspective, rights such as freedom of speech and open elections lose their importance. There are, of course, elections in the Soviet Union; but they perform a different function. The hierarchy of Soviets is directly elected by the people. Voting is much encouraged and there is only one candidate. Nevertheless, the function of the Soviets is more than mere window-dressing. They give an opportunity for participation in politics to citizens who may not be Party members; and they serve to whip up public support for the policies of the state and increase political commitment.

Extensive measures of social control are thought necessary as there are sections of the population whose attitude to the system is at best ambivalent. Most importantly there is the problem of the different nationalities that form the Union of Soviet Socialist Republics. The Soviet Union is an immense country: it is about six thousand miles across and thus Leningrad is nearer to New York than to Vladivostok. It contains twenty-three major nationalities with over a million members each. The largest are the Russians with 129 million, the Ukrainians with forty-one million, the Belorussians and Uzbeks with nine millions each, the Tartars with six million and the Kazakhs with five million. In official theory, these many national groups are merging to form one united *Soviet* nation. Nevertheless, there is considerable unrest among some of the nationalities over what they see as the subordination of their national and cultural interests to those of the specifically Russian section of the Soviet Union. This is particularly so among the Ukrainians. The central (Russian) authorities have certainly allowed inconsistencies to continue. The Baltic republics of Lithuania, Estonia and Latvia, for example, enjoy a higher standard of living than the rest of the Soviet Union. The southern republics of Azerbaidzhan, Georgia, and Armenia have a more relaxed attitude to official controls. And the Soviet authorities have, in general, done much to preserve local culture in the narrow sense of the word. Nevertheless, Moscow retains a firm control. This is achieved partly through the economic division of labour imposed on the Republics through the Plan. Many of the Republics are thereby forced to concentrate on a single product – for example, cotton in Uzbekistan – and are thus rendered more dependent on imports from the rest of the Union. It has also been Moscow's policy to foster specifically Russian immigration into the outlying areas. With almost all specialist technical education being in Russian, the grip of the Russian language is inevitably being extended. Although the First Secretary of the Communist Party in the various republics is usually of the local nationality, the Second Secretary is almost invariably a Russian. Since the birthrate has increased far more rapidly in the outlying Republics, ethnic Russians have recently come to comprise less than half the population. And given the recent upheavals in Iran and Afghanistan, both of which border the Soviet Union, the Moscow authorities will be looking to tighten their grip on their substantial Muslim minorities.

The Jews are a constant problem to the Soviet authorities. The Soviet census counts about two million Jews, but there are probably many more. In the aftermath of the revolution in which they had played such a prominent role, Jewish culture enjoyed a mild revival. With the purges of Stalin and the growth of Russian nationalism, this revival was crushed and turned into outright persecution in Stalin's later years. Today, although many Jews have achieved eminence in the arts and sciences, this is not matched by a corresponding role in the Party; and there is much latent anti-semitism. The surprising privilege of emigration (accorded to no other Soviet citizens) has resulted, in the 1970s, in the departure to Israel of more than 100,000 Jews.

A second area of disaffection in the Soviet state is that of religion. There are twice as many Church members in the Soviet Union as there are members of the Communist Party. About half the babies are baptised and the Churches – those that are left – are packed on holy days. The Orthodox Church was severely repressed in the 1920s and 1930s and then suddenly rehabilitated by Stalin as part of his effort to rally Russian patriotism in the face of Hitler. Krushchev, more liberal in other matters, once again suppressed religious activities and closed three-quarters of the churches. Religion in general has been undergoing a modest revival over the last decade. The Orthodox Church has traditionally been subservient to the state and continues to be so. But the half-a-million Baptists and the Catholics of Lithuania and the Ukraine are often more outspoken.

The third area in which the government encounters opposition, and the best known in the West, is the dissident movement. This movement started in the mid-1960s and was first given shape by the trial in 1966 of the writers Daniel and Sinyavsky for publishing abroad and under pseudonyms what were called 'anti-Soviet' views. There was considerable organised protest following their conviction. The letters, petitions and circulars thus produced were distributed among fellow-sympathisers, giving birth to *samizdat* – literally 'self-published' – literature. Although its main focus is the infringement by the Soviet government of citizens' rights, the dissident movement is extremely diverse. There are those such as the Medvedev brothers, Roy and Zhores, who appeal to what they see as genuine Marxist principles in their criticism of the Soviet régime. The nuclear scientist Andrei Sakharov

An Orthodox service in the Soviet Union. Religion is undergoing a modest revival: there are more members of the Church than of the Party

would like to see the Soviet Union move nearer to a social democratic government of the Western type. Solzhenitsyn, on the other hand, has as little time for what he considers the shallow materialism of the West as he does for the 'superficial economic theory' of Marxism. Solzhenitsyn is a reactionary in the original sense of the word: opposed to modern technology, he wishes to see a return to the spiritual values inherent in Russian village life in a manner strikingly reminiscent of Tolstoy. He is a traditional Christian and a nationalist with a distinctly authoritarian streak. The strength of the dissident movement has, at least for the moment, passed its peak. The steady pressure of persecution – including exile abroad for some, the notorious confinement in mental hospitals for others – has robbed the dissidents of what little influence they possessed in the early 1970s. Moreover, the dissident movement has been confined to a narrow intellectual élite which finds little, if any, support for its views among the masses. The publicity it has received in the West has thus been out of all proportion to its influence.

However irritating the dissident minority may be, the Soviet Union faces far larger problems. Turning to the future, it is apparent that there are three areas of major difficulty.

The first problem is how to keep the revolution alive. The notions of development and progress are at the very core of the Marxist ideology; and each new leader, from Lenin to Brezhnev, has announced a new 'stage' on the road to communism. But the dramatic industrial progress of the earlier decades is now tapering off and Brezhnev's talk of 'developed socialism' fell rather flat. Although Marxist science is inherently predictive, it is paradoxical that the Soviet authorities are extremely chary of predicting anything. There is widespread cynicism and many undoubtedly join the Party not out of belief but in order to further their careers. One indication of social disaffection is the growing problem of alcoholism. Vodka has traditionally been viewed by the Russians as a source of health and warmth. But the Soviet Union has currently the highest per capita consumption of hard liquor in the world. Alcohol is a contributory cause of more than half the crimes and traffic accidents and plays a major role in absenteeism. More generally, the Bolshevik doctrine of the ability of human beings to alter radically their destiny comes into conflict with the Orthodox tradition of not expecting too much from life on this earth. The New Soviet Person finds it hard to incorporate the majority of Russians who, either peasants themselves or at most one or two generations removed from rural life, still retain the easy-going disorganisation and blunt hedonism of their background.

Nevertheless, the spirit of the revolution still has a tangible residue. Most Russians still have a basic confidence in their system. Complain they may, but there is little of the deep cultural pessimism, the profound self-criticism and self-doubt that afflict many Western countries. The optimism that characterised the cultural flowering of the Soviet Union in the 1920s is much more muted now. Nevertheless, there is a widespread view of the Soviet person as the person of the future. This proud individual is projected in novels and television as well as through the educational system. Socialist realism is the order of the day in all arts which are encouraged to be heroic and optimistic. This is particularly striking in Soviet science fiction where the shape of the future contrasts sharply with many of the futile scenarios of the West. The most evident concrete instance of Soviet optimism is the propaganda for Siberia. There is always some heroic project thrust before the public in the Soviet Union, and it is usually in Siberia. Volunteers are collected, through the Young Communist League and other organisations, to help in its construction. Whole cities have sprung up from nothing. For there are almost limitless resources to be tapped: the largest supply of natural gas in the world, huge fields of coal and oil, gold, diamonds and other precious minerals. Life in the Siberian permafrost is tough and a spirit of pioneering idealism prevails among the volunteers. The development of Siberia is a symbol of Soviet progress, a tangible evidence of 'building communism'.

Ultimately, the revolution can only be kept alive through economic success, and this involves the second area of difficulty: increasing the level of the productive forces. Since the industrial base that the Bolsheviks inherited from Tsarist times was small, the progress since achieved has been all the greater. But the post-Stalinist modification of the emphasis on producer goods has created problems. 1953 was the first year in which the rate of production of consumer goods (though not the quantity) began to overtake that of heavy industry. But it was the crash programme in heavy industry that justified the rigidly centralised political system. With the major task of rapid industrialisation now being completed, demands for a system more congruent with the immediate needs of the people are likely to arise. This has happened much more in Eastern Europe than in the Soviet Union where, still, the government is more successful in persuading people to defer their gratifications than in any other industrial society. At present, the domination of producer over consumer goods still continues.

Having successfully negotiated the first industrial revolution, the Soviet Union is faced with coping with the second – and no Stalin is there to provide a ready, if brutal, solution. Soviet achievements in space – from the 1957 Sputnik onwards – are liable to be misleading about the general level of Soviet science and technology. In selected areas – theoretical and particularly nuclear physics, for example – Soviet science is very good. But there are large gaps in, for example, organic chemistry and biology – particularly the genetic engineering which is such a growth area in the West. The Soviet Union puts an enormous emphasis on science and trains more scientists than any other country, but there are few centres of excellence. The Soviet Union has collected far fewer Nobel prizes than Britain, let alone the United States. This is largely due, again, to the general backwardness of the Soviet economy. There is a vicious circle in that science requires an advanced industry to provide it with its materials but advanced industry is also the product of scientific achievement. In the vital field of computerisation – where the Soviet Union is far behind – this is likely to have far-reaching consequences. Nor is scientific progress enhanced by the difficulty of international contact, the bureaucratic controls, and enthusiasm for official secrecy.

The third area of difficulty – the failure of Soviet agriculture – is also the most evident and the one in which the Stalinist legacy has played the predominant role. The collectivisation campaign of the early 1930s had left the countryside in a battered state which continued throughout the Stalinist

This picture is of a state farm in Kazakhstan, the redeeming of whose 'Virgin Lands' was Krushchev's greatest failure

period. The savage campaign waged against the *kulaks* meant that only the poorest and least successful peasants remained. The rate of growth in agricultural production came nowhere near that in industry which commanded all the major investment. The personnel of the Machine and Tractor Stations were used just as much to back up the inadequate Party control as in their ostensible function of supplying equipment to the collective farms. In the capitalist West, the countryside tends to be over-represented politically and hence there is a net transfer of resources from the towns to the country. But all that Stalin was interested in was using the countryside as a source of surplus and steady supply of food for the town; and as the peasant population decreased after the war even this became difficult. Krushchev, by contrast, had a real enthusiasm for agriculture and launched a big drive to cultivate the 'Virgin Lands' of Kazakhstan. Although at first successful, these territories were quickly over-exploited and, as in the early years of American agriculture, some areas became virtual dustbowls.

Under Brezhnev, the progress of the rural sector was steady, but it still faces intractable problems: the Soviet Union for all its size and large numbers employed in agriculture still regularly has to import food. Paradoxically, there are too many people employed on the land – almost a third of the population. In all other highly-industrialised countries, only half that proportion produce enough food for all the rest. More fundamentally, the Soviet Union simply does not possess the industrial base of machines, transport and fertiliser production that efficient modern farming requires. It also lacks the output of consumer goods that would act as an incentive to farmers. A symptom of this weak industrial investment has been the tendency simply to extend the acreage rather than increase the intensity of exploitation. The distribution of agricultural products is also poor in that the same periodic chaos, inefficiency and bottlenecks that characterise the Plan in general also affect agricultural outlets. As a result, the collective farm is by far the least popular of all Soviet institutions and the one most people would like to see changed. There is a gradual drift to the towns, which enjoy a substantially higher standard of living, and inevitably the less enterprising are left behind. The 1981 harvest is widely believed to have been as much as a third short of its target. The US grain embargo following the Soviet invasion of Afghanistan demonstrates that the weakness of Soviet agriculture is a political as well as an economic problem.

The only thriving sector in Soviet agriculture are the many small private plots. These plots only amount to between one and two per cent of the cultivated land, but yield about thirty per cent of the total value distributed through thousands of markets across the country – a form of private enterprise unique in the Soviet Union. Of course, these statistics are partly explicable in terms of peasants getting higher prices for their private produce than those in the state-controlled sector; and the main products of the collective and state farms are the big crops of grain and cotton. But they do nevertheless highlight the stagnation of the countryside which is still the legacy of Stalin.

The Soviet economy is slowing down. The impressive growth rate of previous decades can no longer be sustained. No increase in the labour force can be counted on as the birth rate is falling in European Russia, and agriculture, as presently managed, cannot afford to lose more people. The abiding strength of the Soviet economy is that the only mineral resource it needs to import is tin. But these huge reserves of minerals and energy are mostly in Siberia and it is highly questionable whether the Soviet Union will have either the wealth or the technology to exploit them. Trade with the

Politburo members help carry the open coffin of Leonid Brezhnev. From left to right: Tikhonov, Andropov, Chernenko and Gromyko

West can fill some of the gaps but the current arms race inevitably squeezes other forms of investment. There have been proposals for decentralising the economy in a bid to release more productive energy. But most of those in the bureaucratic hierarchy would feel uneasy if they had to assume more responsibility (and possible blame) for decision-making and those at the top would feel their authority was ebbing away. Even more crucially, economic control is also a form of political control and economic liberalisation would inevitably increase the pressure for political reform. In the 1960s it was thought among some commentators that the increase in the Russian standard of living would bring about some form of liberalisation. This has not proved to be the case. Indeed, Stalinism is undergoing a modest revival. This growing reputation of Stalin among ordinary people is nostalgia for the days of powerful leadership when the country was undergoing visible development towards clear goals.

Nevertheless, détente is in the interests of both East and West. The Soviet economy is weak and strongly dependent on the import of Western technology. The world economy is controlled by the West. World trade is conducted in dollars, not in roubles. Russia has no part in the International Monetary Fund or the World Bank on which so many Third World countries are dependent. If the Russians could develop the vast mineral and energy resources of Siberia, everyone would benefit. The controversial importation of Western technology for the Siberian gas pipeline is the most striking reminder that the Soviet Union has a vested interest in Western economic prosperity. Against all ideological principle, the Russians even co-operate with South Africa over the production of gold and diamonds to their mutual benefit. Like most sorts of bears, the Russian one will only attack if it feels its security threatened.

Russian enthusiasm for Western technology and the growth of East-West trade had led some observers to think that this development of trade and communications would bring about a convergence in the Western and Soviet types of society. The scale and complexity of modern industry leads to similar problems, whether under capitalism or communism, and both types of society would have to evolve similar methods of coping with them. On this view, the expansion of television and travel facilities is turning the world into a global village. Similar technology would increasingly reduce the force of divergent ideology. It is true that in general in Western countries, whatever the political complexion of the government, the tendency has been for growing state intervention in economy and society. More importantly, in the Soviet Union, the Utopianism of the revolutionary epoch has given way to a society with an entrenched hierarchy of statuses and élites. Class struggle has receded before the problems of managing an industrialised society. The improvement of living standards, the growing materialism of the Soviet Union and the half-hearted attempts to decentralise economic decision-making seem to support the convergence thesis. Nevertheless, a fundamental divergence still remains: capitalist societies have a two class system with private firms aiming at profit through a market, however much influenced by the state, and a political leadership subject to electoral change; in the Soviet Union, there is a much more unified economic class system (though with an almost infinite variety of status), state ownership, central planning, and a consequent stability of political leadership. And these differences are unlikely to be diminished in the foreseeable future.

The tradition of strong centralised government is very powerful in Russia and has as much to do with history as with communism. Marx himself emphasised how 'the tradition of all the dead generations weighs like a nightmare on the brain of the living'. We know more about Russia now than when Churchill called the country 'a riddle wrapped in a mystery inside an enigma': but the strangeness still remains. And it undoubtedly springs more from the Russianness, than from the Marxism, of Russia. Talking of the deep-seated influence of history on the Russian character and institutions, one of the most stimulating of recent commentators, Hedrick Smith, cites

Yuri Andropov, former head of the KGB, and successor to Brezhnev as General Secretary of the Communist Party of the Soviet Union

the centralised concentration of power, the fetish of rank, the xenophobia of simple people, the futile carping of alienated intelligentsia, the passionate attachment of Russians to Mother Russia, the habitual submission of the masses to the Supreme Leader, and their unquestioned acceptance of the yawning gulf between the Ruler and the Ruled.

The Soviet Union nevertheless claims Marxism as its official creed. How would Marx, from his tomb in Highgate, judge it? If Lenin, its revolutionary founder, would have had some acid comments to pass on the Soviet Union, we can imagine that Marx himself would have had even more. He would undoubtedly consider, as many of his contemporary followers do, that the Soviet Union is a travesty of what he really wanted – an awful example of what can happen and should not. But the Soviet Union, as so many parts of the world in the twentieth century, has outgrown Marx's frame of reference. No doubt he would appreciate the growth of social equality and the standard of living, particularly as compared with the Tsarist Russia that he knew. Nevertheless, the stifling bureaucracy, the nationalism, the strong sense of hierarchy, above all the lack of any real political power in the hands of the workers – all these would be anathema to him. But Marx was a keen historian and quite a strong determinist. And he would reflect on the inevitability of many of these developments given the failure of revolution in the West and the consequent attempt to build up socialism in one backward country. Like the Irishman when asked for directions, Marx would not have started from there in the first place.

5

ONE GOAL, MANY ROADS

Marxism must take on a national form before it can be applied.

Mao Tse-Tung

For historical and economic reasons, the Soviet Union is the dominant power in the Communist world. But it is not the largest. China has four times as many citizens as the Soviet Union. It also has a very distinctive form of Communism. China's Communist leaders have denounced the Soviet Communists for being revisionist, i.e. deviating from the supposedly orthodox Marxist doctrine. For more than twenty years, indeed, China has been in conflict less with the capitalist world than with the Soviet Union, its fellow Communist state: it has even seemed at times to be on the edge of war with its former ally. Since the split between Moscow and Peking, it is no longer the case that there is a single Marxist centre to which most Marxists look. The roots of Marxism in countries across the world are very different – and so are the routes by which they claim to be progressing towards Communism. In this chapter we shall be looking at three Marxist systems which differ widely from the Soviet model and also amongst themselves.

China
The Chinese revolution is above all a peasant revolution. This involves a radical break with the mainstream of Marxism. Marx himself referred to the 'idiocy of rural life' and had little regard for the revolutionary potential of the peasantry. The individualistic conservatism of the Western European peasantry over the last two centuries has certainly supported his pessimism. The Bolsheviks started off with a land programme favourable to the peasantry but, with Stalin's collectivisation, the countryside became no more than an area to be squeezed unmercifully to provide food for the towns and investment for heavy industry. Not so in China. Mao Tse-tung was himself a peasant; the armies he eventually led to power in 1949 were composed of peasants; and agricultural policy has been the main focus of the Chinese Communist Party's concern.

When the Communist Party was founded in Shanghai in 1921, China was in a state of extreme chaos. For the previous two thousand years, China had been a relatively stable society. Dynasties – Han, T'ang, Ming and Manchu – came and went but the fertile, self-sufficient land mass of China enabled the people to enjoy efficient agriculture and a self-centred civilisation imbued with a Confucian philosophy which sanctioned hierarchy and viewed any change as degeneration. This stability was shattered by the encroachment of the Western powers in the mid-nineteenth century. Events from the Opium War of 1840 to the defeat by the previously despised Japanese in 1895 and the suppression of the Boxer rebellion in 1900, revealed China to be almost completely defenceless in the face of economic and military pressure from the West. In 1912, the Manchu dynasty fell and a Republic was proclaimed. But with no emperor to unify the country, only different centres of military power remained, controlled by various warlords whose irregular troops battened on the peasantry, destroyed the economic equilibrium of the countryside, and swept aside for ever the imperial bureaucracy. It was during this unstable period that Chinese Marxism was born.

The Chinese Communists began as orthodox Marxists. This orthodoxy held that the proletariat was the revolutionary class but that in underdeveloped countries the road to proletarian power lay through some kind of preliminary nationalist, republican, bourgeois revolution. In the early 1920s, most revolutionary nationalist forces in China supported the Kuomintang, the political party led by Dr Sun Yat-sen which had succeeded in establishing itself, aided by the Russians, in South China with its headquarters in Canton. In early 1926, the Kuomintang, now under the leadership of Chiang Kai-shek who had succeeded Sun, mounted the Northern Expedition to rid China of the warlords and the Western colonialists who abetted them. The vital question was: what should be the attitude of the Chinese Communist Party to the Kuomintang? Urged on by Stalin, the Chinese Communists decided to join forces with them. But following the success of the Northern Expedition, the warnings of Trotsky proved right. Chiang Kai-shek had no wish to play Kerensky to some Chinese Lenin. He turned on his Communist allies, killed several hundred of them, proscribed the Party, and destroyed its fragile bases in the industrial cities.

Traditional Marxist strategy had thus proved a failure. The Communists had tried to set up bases in the major cities of Canton and Shanghai – much as their Bolshevik mentors had done in Moscow and Petrograd. With these now destroyed, the only recourse was to the countryside. The shattered remnants of the Communist forces retreated to the wild, mountainous regions of the Chingkangshan on the eastern borders of Hunan province. Here Mao Tse-tung came into his own. He had been born in Hunan province in 1893, the son of a poor peasant who became relatively rich from trading in grain.

After studying for many years under adverse conditions, Mao encountered Marxism while working as an assistant librarian in Peking and was one of the founder members of the Communist Party. Given his origins, his antipathy to intellectuals and his ignorance of urban life, Mao quickly became the Party's expert on the peasantry. His unbounded enthusiasm for the revolutionary potential of the peasantry is evident from the visionary beginning of his first important writing on the question:

> The present upsurge of the peasant movement is a colossal event. In a very short time, in China's central, southern and northern provinces, several hundred million peasants will arrive like a mighty storm, like a hurricane, a force so swift and violent that no power, however great, will be able to hold it back. They will smash all the trammels that bind them and rush forward along the road to liberation. They will sweep all the imperialists, warlords, corrupt officials, local tyrants and evil gentry into their graves. Every revolutionary party and every revolutionary comrade will be put to the test, to be accepted or rejected as they decide.

This marked a new departure for Marxist theory. From now on it was the peasantry, not the proletariat, who were to be the vanguard of the revolution.

The retreat to the wild mountains of the Chingkangshan meant the addition of another new element to Mao's Marxism: the Communist Party became essentially a guerilla army. Mao was able to draw on his youthful

The Long March of 1934/5 in which the Red Army travelled 6,000 miles across China to found a permanent base in Yenan province

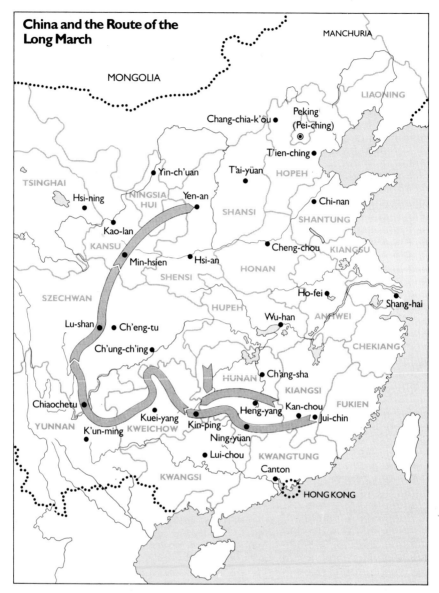

China and the Route of the Long March

reading of classical Chinese novels such as *The Water Margin* with their glorification of peasant revolts and military exploits. It was here that he formulated the now classic tactic of the Red Army:

> The enemy advances, we retreat;
> the enemy halts, we harass;
> the enemy tires, we attack:
> the enemy retreats, we pursue.

However, the Red Army was still small and by 1933 the Kuomintang had encircled the Communist area with block-houses. The only course left to the Red Army was to break out and seek refuge elsewhere. They did so in 1934 and trekked for six thousand miles and twelve months over the most difficult terrain before finding a secure base in Yenan in northwest China. The Long March became the heroic foundation myth of Communist China. It was also the period when Mao became the undisputed leader of the Party.

The base in Yenan proved unassailable and the years 1939 to 1945 saw a steady expansion of Communist power, first in an alliance with the Kuomintang against the Japanese invaders, then in a civil war against the Kuomintang itself. The border regions of Yenan also provided the model for later economic policies. The soldiers and Party officials took part in land reclamation schemes, farming and the development of light industry. The emphasis was on the self-sufficiency necessary for survival and the ethos was democratic, participatory and self-sacrificial. Particularly, co-operatives were established to promote intermediate technology and whole areas were encouraged to band together to provide their own raw materials, rudimentary transport and power supplies, and eventually their own schools and clinics. This provided the model for the later Communes.

The embattled nature of the Communist enclave meant that more emphasis than ever was put on the army. As Mao put it in a famous passage:

> Every Communist must grasp the truth: 'Political power grows out of the barrel of a gun'. Our principle is that the Party commands the gun, and the gun must never be allowed to command the Party. Yet, having guns, we can create Party organisations, as witness the powerful Party organisations which the Eighth Route Army has created in northern China. We can also create cadres, create schools, create culture, create mass movements. Everything in Yenan has been created by having guns. All things grow out of the barrel of a gun.

The final victory of the Communists in 1949 owed much to their social policies. Mao thought it vital that the guerillas should control bases to which they could periodically retire. These should be areas that were geographically difficult of access – mountainous, bordered by swamps or deserts, etc. In these areas, the troops themselves should work the land and be active in production, they should help raise the productivity of the local inhabitants and, if possible, organise elementary social services. This would both avoid their being a burden on the locals and counter the boredom of periodic inactivity that sapped the morale of all traditional armies. The continued emphasis on the importance of political consciousness and of morale, and the theme of men, not weapons, being the decisive factor were characteristic

Mao Tse-tung addressing students in Yenan in 1938

of the Chinese Revolution as a whole. And these were the tactics later applied successfully by Tito's partisans in Yugoslavia, by the FLN in Algeria and, of course, by the Vietcong in Indo-China.

From the above it will be clear that the Chinese Communist Party in 1949 faced a very different situation from that of the Bolsheviks in 1917. Russia was a European power and had had centuries of contact with the ideas and technology of Western Europe with the result that by 1917 there was already a considerable industrial base. China, by contrast, had traditionally been a closed society. Even by 1949 industrial development was nowhere near that of Russia in 1917 as the country had been ravaged by twenty years of invasion and civil war. Whereas in the Soviet Union the relatively short civil war came *after* the revolution, in China the Party came to power after two decades of armed struggle. Finally, the Bolsheviks had their political strength in the working class of the cities where the revolution began: in China the cities were the last to fall to a guerilla army of peasant origin.

Nevertheless, the initial policies of the Chinese government were based upon the model of the Soviet Union, their only ally and exemplar. During their first few years of power, the changes were moderate: most large capitalist enterprises were nationalised (with compensation), but smaller businesses were even encouraged. Land was redistributed to poor peasants, but still on the basis of private property. However, the inevitable clash between planning and private enterprise, and the strains imposed by the Korean War, hastened the progress towards socialism. The first five-year plan of 1953–57 put emphasis on heavy industry and, with the aid of thousands of Soviet technicians to help install and operate the plants, was a success: output of most major sectors doubled in the five years. By the same time, the vast majority of the peasants had been organised into socialist co-operatives in which land and capital was held in common and income allotted according to work done.

By 1958, however, Mao was convinced that a radically new departure was necessary. The growth rate was slowing down and the population began to increase dramatically with economic recovery. Mao's faith in the revolutionary potential of the Chinese countryside and his preference for men over machines led him eventually to think that a rise in agricultural production would have to precede or at least accompany a rise in industrial production. Early in 1958, therefore, he launched the frenetic economic drive that came to be known as the Great Leap Forward. This movement put greater emphasis on agriculture and on mass mobilisation under the general slogan of 'politics in command'. It also marked an abandonment of the Soviet model of investment. The leap consisted principally in diverting the resources of the industrial sector directly into agriculture and thus creating in the villages a real and accelerating process of industrialisation. This was to be achieved by an all-out mobilisation of local surplus labour and the development of local sources of power and raw materials. The most striking aspect of the latter policy was the programme for producing steel in thousands of home-made furnaces across the country.

Side by side with the Great Leap Forward went the collectivisation movement of the Communes. Their slogan was 'Big in scale, common in ownership'. They combined several large co-operatives to form units of about 100,000 people – though the size was extremely variable. During 1958 26,000 Communes took the place of 74,000 advanced co-operatives. This enabled the work force to be directed according to the general need of the Commune: light industry and large-scale agricultural improvements (irrigation, for example) would be facilitated. Communal eating, laundry, nurseries, etc., would release a lot of labour, particularly female, and reduce to a minimum the private property of the peasant. The system of payment was a combination of regard for needs and work contributed. In addition, the Commune was to become the basic unit of local government. As with the Great Leap Forward, the Commune movement was an attempt to achieve the growth of agriculture needed to sustain industry and increase exports. Like Bukharin, Mao believed that industry should serve agriculture and he promoted the Communes in order to foster peasant accumulation –

Members of a Commune terracing a hillside to make it suitable for rice growing and below, the finished result

not in order to extract the surplus for the benefit of heavy industry like Stalin.

In the event, the Great Leap Forward was a dramatic failure. The scale of the failure and of the ensuing widespread starvation is only becoming gradually clear from bits of information released in the post-Mao period. The price to be paid for the growing divergence from the Soviet Union was the withdrawal, virtually overnight, of all Russian aid and experts in 1960. Bad luck also played a part as 1959–61 saw the worst drought and floods within living memory. The hasty transition to collective property aroused deep and bitter resentment among the peasants and the lack of overall co-ordination meant many bottlenecks and shortages. Although the upheaval was not comparable to the Stalinist collectivisation, the clumsy imposition of socialism in the countryside did arouse considerable opposition. Even Mao himself had to admit that 'we over-estimated the enthusiasm of the peasants'. Again unlike Stalin, the government did not press on regardless but moved back to something much more like the Russian New Economic Policy. Material incentives were reintroduced, the market was given a greater role, and private landholding admitted.

But Mao, little daunted, was only biding his time before unleashing the even more profound shake-up of the system known as the Great Proletarian Cultural Revolution. Fundamental to Mao's political thought was his idea that conflict was inherent and creative even in socialist society. He sometimes referred to this idea as 'permanent revolution' but thereby went far beyond Marx who confined this expression to conflict *before* a socialist revolution. For Mao, however, conflict within socialist society was, within limits, to be encouraged. Mao summed this up by saying that in his dialectic 'one divides into two' producing healthy contradiction and thereby progress; the Soviet dialectic of 'two divides into one' produced only a fossilised conformism. Already in 1957 Mao had promoted this idea under the slogan 'let a hundred flowers bloom and a hundred schools of thought contend'. The resulting waves of criticism, however, particularly from leaders of minority parties and from universities and intellectuals in general, alarmed the leadership. And very soon extremely strict criteria were formulated to distinguish the 'fragrant flowers' from the 'poisonous weeds'.

The initial aim of the Cultural Revolution was to halt the drift away from socialism following the failures of 1958/59, to challenge the entrenchment of the bureaucracy, and to attack 'those within the Party who are in authority and are taking the capitalist road'. It was the final effort of Mao the revolutionary romantic to challenge the hierarchical, specialised and bureaucratic institutions that seemed to be entailed by China's economic and political development. It was a return to the mentality of the successful pre-

A landlord farmer awaits execution after appearing before a People's
Court and charged with exploiting the peasants

war Yenan days with the attempt to break down the distinction between
mental and manual labour, between industry and agriculture, between town
and country. The subsequent attack on the authority of the Party as an
institution was unprecedented in the history of the Communist movement.

The two most prominent aspects of the Cultural Revolution were the
activities of the Red Guards and the promotion of Mao's Little Red Book.
The Red Guard movement was launched by Mao and his heir-apparent Lin
Piao in an effort to oust the 'capitalist roaders' Liu Shao-Ch'i and Deng
Xiaoping. But the movement very soon acquired its own momentum.
The Red Guards were mostly students whose lack of experience of pre-
Communist misery made them readier to criticise present policies and
whose absence from the universities would not be immediately damaging to
the economy. They organised huge demonstrations in Peking; they went on
long journeys in teams to help in production and participate in the autumn
harvest; and wherever they went they emphasised the importance of the
masses who should make themselves felt, freedom to criticise, opposition to
all conservatives, and the right to rebel. The one guideline was loyalty to
Mao Tse-tung's thought as expressed in the Little Red Book. The dislocation
in the governmental apparatus in the educational system, and in the economy

in general was immense. Universities closed, and so did schools. Managers, technical experts, teachers and others were disgraced, humiliated and some killed. Industry had almost come to a halt. When the authority of the Party itself was put in jeopardy, even Mao began to have second thoughts. His dilemma was vividly expressed in his unscripted remarks in 1967 following the proclamation of a People's Commune in Shanghai:

> If all [of these organisations] are changed into communes, what will we do with the Party? Where will we put the Party? In the committees set up under a commune, there will be members who belong to the Party, and others who don't. Where will we put the Party committee? . . . There has to be a nucleus. It doesn't matter what it's called, it is all right to call it a Communist Party, it is all right to call it a social-democratic party, it is all right to call it a social-democratic workers' party, it is all right to call it a Kuomintang, it is all right to call it the I-kuan-tao, but in any case there has to be a party. In a commune there has to be a party; can the commune replace the Party?

The shaking up of the old bureaucracy and the mutual hostility and transitory nature of many of the rebel groupings thrown up by the Cultural Revolution left a power vacuum that could only be filled by the People's Liberation Army which was a fairly cohesive and unified body. In the summer of 1968, the Red Guards were disbanded and the Ninth Congress in 1969 re-established Party control. Almost half of the members of the new Central Committee were from the Army and the powers of the Politburo were increased. The ascendancy of Mao had passed its zenith.

For all its talk of mass participation (which does have some reality in the grass roots economy) the Chinese Communist Party is an extraordinarily authoritarian organisation. Like any other Communist Party, the Chinese adheres to the Leninist doctrine of democratic centralism. But the long military struggle in which it was engaged meant that the Party leant more to centralism than to democracy. In a speech of 1942, Mao said of certain comrades:

> they do not understand the Party's system of democratic centralism; they do not realise that the Communist Party not only needs democracy but needs centralisation even more. They forget the system of democratic centralism in which the minority is subordinate to the majority, the lower level to the higher level, the part to the whole and the entire membership to the Central Committee.

The centralised nature of the Party is matched by a strong paternalism towards 'the masses'. Indeed, the very backwardness of China (which meant

The rice harvest on a Commune. China has difficulty raising agricultural production to keep pace with a growing population

that initiatives would have to come from the Party) was held by Mao to be an advantage. He believed strongly in the malleability of human nature and considered the Chinese people to be more malleable than most:

> China's 600 million people have two remarkable peculiarities; they are, first of all, poor and, secondly, blank. That may seem like a bad thing, but it is really a good thing. Poor people want change, want to do things, want revolution. A clean sheet of paper has no blotches, and so the newest and most beautiful words can be written on it, the newest and most beautiful pictures can be painted on it.

This did not, however, preclude the consultation of these same masses. Mao insisted that good communication was essential in order to provide the leadership with the raw material on which they had to go to work. Neverthe-less, the initiatives of the masses tended not to be well received if they were regarded as not being impregnated with Mao Tse-tung's thought – as in some aspects of the Cultural Revolution.

Even more than in the Soviet Union, power is concentrated in the Chinese Politburo. The Politburo is elected by the full Central Committee. But the Central Committee meets only infrequently – it did not meet at all for example, from September 1962 to August 1966 and is sometimes called upon to ratify retrospectively important decisions taken by the Politburo that have been in force for a long time. The same applies to Party Congresses: there was only one between 1945 and 1969. Any form of participatory democ-racy is rendered impossible by the immense cloak of secrecy surrounding all deliberations at the top of the Chinese Communist Party. This is not to say that there have not been serious differences of opinion within the Party which is certainly no monolith. Mao himself was never simply a dictator: many of his Party colleagues enjoyed revolutionary reputations in their own right and Mao had sometimes to resort to playing one off against another or even to promoting extra-Party campaigns to get his point of view across.

Maoism died before Mao himself. It could not survive the setback of the Cultural Revolution. Mao lingered on, a tragic figure, until 1976. But Lin Piao, his closest colleague and designated successor, was accused of trying to establish 'a feudal-fascist dictatorship' and perished in an air crash in 1971 while allegedly attempting to flee to the Soviet Union. Two years later, Deng Xiaoping was restored to high office. Deng, currently the most in-fluential of Chinese politicians, had been viewed as an arch-traitor during the Cultural Revolution for proclaiming that hard work, not politics, should be in command. He was credited with the very unideological view that 'it doesn't matter what colour the cat is, so long as it catches mice'. In 1976, a year which saw the death of Premier Chou En-lai as well as that of Mao, it looked for a moment as though the 'Gang of Four' would gain control. The four, who included Mao's widow Chiang Ch'ing, had been prominent in the Cultural Revolution. Deng was demoted, but a few months later the Party Central Committee confirmed that the colourless Hua Quo-feng would become Party chairman. The Gang of Four were arrested and Deng, the original rubber man, bounced back to the centre of power where he remained. His influence as the most powerful figure in a more or less collective leader-ship was confirmed by the Twelfth Party Congress in 1982. In 1978 a flurry of wall posters appeared in Peking containing the most diverse viewpoints and generally advocating more open debate, democracy, and free speech. But this was too much for the leadership and the 'democracy walls' were abruptly halted the following year.

Wall posters were a great feature of the Cultural Revolution of 1966–69.
The 'democracy walls' of 1980 seen here have recently been severely
curtailed by the government

Underlying these upheavals in the political leadership has been a steady retreat from the principles of the Cultural Revolution. The emphasis now is on discipline, material incentives and specialisation. Central planning has been reinforced and 'expert' is given preference over 'red'. In many respects, the Gang of Four were conservatives: now the watchword is modernisation in the key sectors of industry, agriculture, science and defence. This change is particularly striking in two areas. Firstly, the denigration of foreigners characteristic of the Cultural Revolution has given way to a cautious admittance of imported technology – particularly from Japan which is increasingly fulfilling the same economic role towards China as the Soviet Union did in the 1950s. Secondly, it is clear that in agriculture the spirit of Bukharin lives again. The People's Communes are being effectively dismantled and schemes are being tried out which allow each household to farm a plot of land and, after taxes and contributions to collective projects, keep the surplus for itself. The general change of emphasis has been reflected in China's new constitutions of 1978 and 1982. The 1978 Constitution, while paying lip service to Mao, emphasised the Party's task of conciliation, mentioned the importance of material rewards, and stressed modernisation. The 1982 Constitution broadens State and Party control, and restores a strong measure of local government separate from the disintegrating Communes. But however much the economic policies of Mao may have been modified, the authoritarian paternalism is still there. China is, after all, the country that *invented* the bureaucratic élite. Even after the Cultural Revolution, well over half the members of the Central Committee had entered the Party before 1928 and the average age of the Politburo is sixty-five. Deng will celebrate his eightieth birthday in 1984. The military are well represented in the Party hierarchy but, unlike the Soviet Union, there are few with a managerial or technical background.

In spite of the political upheavals of recent years, China has maintained an impressive rate of economic growth – about eight per cent per annum of industrial output. However, it is easy to forget that China was and remains an extremely poor country. The value of what even an average Russian produces is ten times that of an average Chinese. This backwardness and poverty creates enormous difficulties. The importing of foreign technology is neither cheap nor simple. And modernisation requires a greater degree of openness than has hitherto characterised Chinese society. The current purge of those who rose to power during the Cultural Revolution is likely further to discourage initiative among a bureaucracy whose chief aim becomes simply keeping their jobs. Although the vast majority of the Chinese are well fed, there remain substantial pockets of malnutrition. China's greatest problem is simply to ensure that the growth in the economy is not outstripped by that in the population which has just passed the thousand million mark.

For all its size, China and its revolution has had surprisingly little effect on the rest of the world. Undoubtedly the dominant theme in China's relationship to the outside world is its hostility to the Soviet Union. This has a lengthy history in that the young Soviet Republic filched, on the Chinese view, vast territories in Manchuria and Mongolia which were properly part of China. Indeed, the Sino-Soviet split largely accounts for China's hostility to Vietnam (culminating in actual invasion in December 1978) and her support for the murderous Pol Pot régime in Cambodia. Ideologically, too, Mao was an incipient heretic in Marxist-Leninist terms as far back as 1927 when he espoused the notion of a nationalist revolution founded in the peasantry. Nevertheless, until the death of Stalin, Mao asserted that all countries, including China, were destined to travel the same revolutionary path as the Soviet Union. With the consolidation of Krushchev's position, however, the Chinese claimed to see a restoration of capitalism in the Soviet Union. Krushchev's idea of the USSR as a 'state of the whole people' seemed to the Chinese to negate the dictatorship of the proletariat and the necessity of continued class struggle during the transition to communism. Krushchev was also accused of revising both Lenin's theory of imperialism and his doctrine of war and peace. The idea of peaceful coexistence was denounced as a cloak for the dividing up of world influence between the two superpowers.

The quarrel between China and the Soviet Union – sharpened by actual border clashes in 1969 – meant that China's foreign policy underwent a radical transformation. The view that the Soviet Union was a greater enemy than the United States had far-reaching consequences. From the early 1970s the Chinese tended to view the world more in terms of two superpowers seeking world domination than in traditional Left/Right terms. Indeed, China currently has a foreign policy well to the right of the Soviet Union. In the early 1970s it seemed that the more 'radical' the internal policies of the Chinese government, the less socialist was its foreign policy. Following Lin Piao's classic formula that the 'cities of the world' (North America and Western Europe) would be encircled and conquered by the 'countryside' of Asia, Africa and Latin America, Chinese aid had been given to many revolutionary movements around the world during the 1960s. But with the emergence of the view that the Soviet Union was an imperialist power, Chinese foreign policy took on a novel form. China supported, both morally and economically, armed repression by the Pakistani military government of Leftist dissidents prior to the establishment of Bangladesh. In April 1971 they supported similar measures by the Bandaranaike government in Ceylon. This change in policy was symbolised by the visit of President Nixon to

Mao and Krushchev in Peking in 1958. Two years later the Sino-Soviet
split occurred and the Communist world has remained divided ever since

Peking only two months after the mining of Haiphong Harbour. Peking was
quick to recognise the military junta that overthrew President Allende in
Chile and even gave it limited moral support. During the Civil War in
Angola the Chinese found themselves supporting the CIA-backed FNLA
against the Moscow-orientated Marxists. These extraordinary attitudes can
only be explained on the far-fetched assumption that Soviet 'social imperialism' is the greatest threat to socialist revolution the world over.

Yugoslavia and Eastern Europe
China is not the only Communist country to criticise the Soviet Union.
Nearer home and better informed, Yugoslavia has evolved over the last
thirty years a very different sort of socialism from that of the Soviets. They
have insisted that there are several different roads to communism and rejected the Soviet model as too centralised and bureaucratic. Their ability to
do this has been due partly to the lack of any direct threat from the Soviet
Union and partly to the way in which the Yugoslav Communists came to
power after the Second World War.

The Yugoslav Communist Party was not always so independently minded.
During the 1930s, Yugoslavia had been ruled by an absolute monarchy and
the Communist Party rigorously suppressed. It survived, however, to become the nucleus of a guerilla movement and then an army resisting German
occupation. Unlike other régimes in Eastern Europe, the Communists in
Yugoslavia owed their power after the war to their own efforts as a resistance

President Tito and his wife. The Yugoslav self-management system evolved under Tito is markedly different from the Soviet model

movement and not to the support of Russian tanks. They also enjoyed, in Josip Broz (who adopted the name Tito during the war), a leader of exceptional political ability. Born of peasant parents, Tito abandoned his original ambition to be a tailor (he was always most careful of his appearance) to become a full-time Party worker and then General Secretary in 1939. Paternalist, empathetic, and decisive, Tito remained the unchallenged monarch of Yugoslav Communism until his death in 1980.

Although from the start Tito enhanced the independence of the Yugoslav Party by refusing aid from the Comintern, he began as a completely orthodox Marxist of the Soviet type. During and immediately after the Second World War there were no more enthusiastic admirers of Stalin and copiers of Soviet institutions than Tito and his followers. Until 1948, Yugoslavia was a model satellite. The break with the Soviet Union was initially caused by Yugoslav attempts to resist increasing Soviet tutelage, a resistance which resulted in their expulsion from the Communist fraternity. The immediate reaction of the Yugoslavs was to prove themselves even more orthodox by attempting to collectivise agriculture which they had not done before owing to the strong peasant base of the Party and the resistance movement. But in face of continued Soviet hostility, the régime embarked in 1952/53 on a dramatically new model of socialism.

This Yugoslav model had two parts to it: a dismantling of the centralised structures of Party and State, and a system of workers' self-management with strong emphasis on the role of market forces. Yugoslavia is the one Communist State to have taken seriously the idea of its own withering away. The reforms of 1952/53 explicitly referred back to Marx's praise of the Paris Commune. The Party programme stated:

> As the socialist democratic system develops, the role of the state administration begins to diminish in the direct management of the economy, in the field of cultural and educational activities, the health service and social policy, etc. The functions connected with the administration of these activities are increasingly transferred to various social self-governing bodies, which are independent or linked up into a suitable democratic organisational machinery.

In accordance with this aim, much power was devolved away from central government to local councils, considerable use was made of referenda, and an attempt made, by the frequent rotation of office holders, to avoid a class of professional politicians emerging, at least at the local level. Naturally, this model of participatory democracy could only be something more than a façade if the role of the Party was also modified to the extent of abandoning its traditional Leninist structure. Symbolically, the name was changed from

Communist Party to League of Communists and its directing role minimised. Although the Communists did not completely abandon their 'leading role', the programme stated that this role was to be fulfilled 'less and less
by their own power and more and more by means of the direct power of the
working people who operate the socially-owned means of production and by
means of the most variegated forms of social self-government'.

This political decentralisation has been based on a fundamental reorganisation of the economy and a new idea of socialist property. According
to the Yugoslavs, state ownership was not sufficient to achieve socialism:
indeed, it would be accompanied by disaffection of the workers and inequality unless there were also some form of real participation and control from
below. Marx had talked of 'an association of free producers'; and the Yugoslavs went some way towards this by creating a system of workers' self-
management in which control of enterprises was vested in a workers' council
elected by all members of the enterprise. The council in turn elects the
managing board. Since 1965, the Council is the sovereign body in the enterprise: it cannot sell the property of the enterprise, but it is responsible for
planning production, fixing prices and wages and determining investment.

Yugoslavia's experiments have come in for a lot of criticism from its
socialist neighbours. The problems of a transition from capitalism to socialism are long and arduous, they say; Yugoslavia has shown that a transition
from socialism to capitalism is only too easy. The undermining of a centrally
planned economy and the reintroduction of 'profit' as a criterion of the success of enterprises is tantamount to the abandonment of socialism: the competition between enterprises means the re-emergence of inequality (with
managers effectively operating as a bureaucratic bourgeoisie) and the neg-
lect of the needs of society as a whole. From a Leninist point of view, the
granting of power to workers' councils smacks of the kind of syndicalist
workers' power or even anarchism that Lenin himself did so much to
combat.

Another sort of criticism of the Yugoslav system is that the real power of
the workers' council is much less than it seems and that the complexity
of business and technological sophistication mean that effective decision-
making still rests with the management. Insofar as the councils serve to
promote the feeling of a common aim, they actually render the manager's
job all the easier by integrating the workers into the industrial system. The
inequalities between rich and poor regions have been intensified, and inevitably the problems such as inflation and unemployment, that so plague
Western capitalist economies, have also emerged in Yugoslavia.

Nor has the League of Communists been united in its approach to decentralisation. Milovan Dijlas, once a close friend to Tito and author of *The*

New Class, a wholesale attack on bureaucratic Marxism, wished the powers of the League to be even further decreased and publicly attacked the life-style of League members. He has been under house arrest ever since. On the other side, Aleksander Rankovic, who had been Tito's right-hand man and probable successor, was bent on reasserting a party of the Leninist or even Stalinist type. Following his disgrace in 1966, central control was relaxed even further and the policies of the League became increasingly vague.

During the 1970s, economic and social self-management has been pre-served and even in some cases increased. But the political control from the centre has been re-asserted. This is largely because the lack of central con-trol permitted an unacceptable degree of regional nationalism to assert itself. Yugoslavia is a difficult country to keep together at the best of times with eighteen ethnic groups, six nationalities and three religions. The economic reforms have encouraged nationalism particularly in Croatia which wanted to keep for itself the enormous sums earned from foreign tourists and felt in general that its traditionally higher standard of living was being jeopardised to the benefit of the Serbian majority who also controlled the capital Belgrade. Only Tito, himself the product of a mixed marriage between a Croatian father and a Serbian mother, was able to maintain the League's central control through a drastic purge of the Croatian and Serbian leader-ship.

Tito had been the effective monarch of his new state for thirty-five years. With his death in May 1980, the leadership has been rotated under a system devised by Tito himself 'to prevent', as he put it, 'a Stalin emerging after my Lenin'. It had been his ambition to turn his country into a sort of socialist Switzerland – neutral, federalist and democratic. In the post-Tito era it will be difficult for the leadership to keep the nationalities in check, as the recent disturbances among the Albanian minority in the southern province of Kosovo demonstrates. Already in the mid-1970s there was a swing away from liberal freedoms with a tightening of pressure on academic and pub-lishing institutions – though Yugoslavs enjoy a cultural tolerance unknown in any other Eastern bloc country. With the general economic recession and inflation at around thirty per cent, it will be difficult to tighten controls without alienating nationalist sentiment, damaging vital Western economic support, and undermining the very system of self-management which is the régime's proudest boast.

Yugoslavia is the only East European country to have escaped the Soviet orbit. Nevertheless, the common Marxism-Leninism of the Soviet satellites is very diversely interpreted. Nearest in style to Yugoslavia is Hungary whose economy represents an island of comparative prosperity in the Com-munist bloc. This has been achieved under the rule of Janos Kadar whose

This massive fallen head of Stalin in the centre of Budapest during the
1956 uprising, symbolises the anti-Soviet feeling of the times

role as Soviet front man in crushing the 1956 rising made him feared and
reviled in his own country. Today, he is one of the few Communist leaders
who could be sure of winning power in a free election. Over the last twenty
years, the Hungarian Communist Party has quietly been building up a
mood of reconciliation within the country based on Kadar's statement that
'Those who are not against us are with us'. There is greater freedom of
expression; travel to the West is permitted; and religious practice is not
persecuted. The leading role of the Party has remained sacrosanct but it has
been exercised very pragmatically as Hungary's socialist economy – a long
time member of the IMF – gives ample room for private enterprise and
profit.

Czechoslovakia, by contrast, has not recovered from the reaction to the
Prague Spring of 1968. Whereas the Hungarian revolt of 1956 had its
origins outside the Party and was directed against Communist rule, the
Czech reform movement started inside the Party with the election of Dubcek
as First Secretary in January 1968. The Czechoslovak Communist Party
was the only mass Communist Party in Eastern Europe before the war and
obtained nearly forty per cent of the vote in the last free elections in 1946.
The libertarian Marxism of 1968 thus marked a return to the pre-war Czech

A week after the Warsaw Pact invasion of Czechoslavakia in August 1968. The slogan draws a stark parallel between the Americans in Vietnam and Russians in Czechoslavakia

political culture and a reaction to the previous Novotny regime, the only East European government to preserve Stalinism through into the 1960s. The Czech 'Socialism with a human face' had deep roots in Party and State. The Husak regime and the 'normalisation' that followed the Warsaw Pact invasion could only re-establish control by imposing the most rigid kind of centralisation.

Poland is different yet again in that the strong position of the Catholic Church and the fact that the important agricultural sector remained in private hands has always provided an alternative to Communist values. Traditional hostility to Russia and the imposition of Communist rule by the Red Army got the government off to a bad start. The Communist authorities had an ideological prejudice against the agricultural sector which they had briefly tried to collectivise in the 1950s. Yielding to privatisation with bad grace, they starved the farms of investment and prevented peasants buying each other out and thus creating larger and more efficient units. The attempt to develop Polish industry under Gierek by borrowing hugely from the West was stopped short by the oil crisis of 1973/4 and difficulties compounded by subsequent high interest rates. Corruption in the Party hierarchy together with dramatic mismanagement of the economy led to the

The grass roots and informal nature of Solidarity is well conveyed in this picture of Lech Walesa discussing strategy with his colleagues on the National Committee

emergence of the non-Communist trade union movement Solidarity. It was not so much Solidarity's economic power as its political challenge to the leading role of the Party that brought about the imposition of martial law in December 1981. The visible fact that the Army, and not the discredited Party, was now in power removed even the fig-leaf of ideological justification for the régime.

Perhaps the most curious of East European régimes is that of Rumania. Its relative independence in foreign policy and willingness to distance itself from the Soviet Union has endeared Rumania to some Western minds. From the early 1960s, an effective campaign of de-Sovietisation has been waged, with the restoration of Rumanian street names previously Russified and emphasis on pre-Communist national heroes. In 1964 the Rumanians gave added impetus to this campaign by publishing Marx's hitherto unknown *Notes on the Rumanians*. Although of little intrinsic interest, they did contain a fair sample of Marx's invective against (Tsarist) Russia as a dangerously predatory imperialist country. This independent foreign policy is accompanied at home by very harsh governmental repression. Power is also kept well within the family: of the nine people in the ruling Permanent Bureau, four are close relatives of President Ceaucescu – himself the object of a considerable personality cult.

Diverse though they may be, the East European Communist régimes have in common the fact that, unlike Yugoslavia, they owe their origins to the backing of the Russian army in the immediate post-war years. And this continues to be true, although less directly, today – as the recent Polish experience demonstrates. It is ironical that the fate of the Bolshevik revolution, in their own minds and also in reality, was dependent on what happened in the rest of Europe. Today, the dependency is reversed, and what is possible in Eastern Europe is largely determined by the Soviet Union.

Cuba

The Cuban revolution which brought Fidel Castro and his followers to power in 1959 was strikingly different from previous Marxist models. The initiative for the Cuban revolution came neither from the working class nor from the Communist Party. Unlike either China or the Soviet Union, Cuba was more urban than rural and was not plagued by deep social division or extreme widespread poverty. On almost any criterion, Cuba was one of the most developed countries in Latin America and the organised section of the working class enjoyed a comparatively high standard of living. What made Cuban society unstable was the extraordinarily high rate of unemployment and the parasitic nature of the upper classes who derived their considerable wealth from rents, excessive profits, tax evasion and more sinister forms of corruption. Although granted independence from Spain in 1902, Cuba was subject to constant diplomatic, economic and even military pressure from the United States. American influence was fostered by the rule of Batista who had been in power (apart from a break in the immediate post-war period) since 1933. The authoritarian nature of the government, the dependency on American capitalism, and the predominance of the sugar industry, meant that there was no independent and stable middle class. In its origins, the Cuban revolution was a nationalist rebellion by disaffected youth (Castro was only thirty-two on attaining power) against a corrupt régime which depended largely on foreign support. Castro and his followers drew their original inspiration from the traditional liberation movements against Spain and the United States that had little to do with socialism. Their main quarrel was with President Batista and his reliance on 'The Colossus of the North'.

Initially, Castro's attempt to overthrow the Batista dictatorship seemed to have little chance of success. Batista's return to power in 1952 persuaded Castro, a law graduate and son of a prosperous landowner, to give up his career inside the system and turn to insurrection. He led a ludicrously ill-prepared assault on the Moncada barracks (the largest in the country) in 1953. Sentenced to fifteen years in prison, he benefited from a general amnesty after less than two years, went to Mexico, bought a yacht, the

Granma, and landed in Cuba at the end of 1956. Of the original eighty-two men, only sixteen survived attacks from the Batista forces and fled to the Sierra Maestra mountains to continue the struggle. After withstanding assaults from government troops, the guerillas began to infiltrate the plains. Their task was made the easier by the corruption and brutality of the Batista army. Castro and his forces entered Havana on 1 January 1959, exactly two years and one month after the *Granma* landing.

Following the triumph of the *Fidelistas*, Cuba adopted a neutral foreign policy and a reformist internal policy which tried to attract private investment. The growing nationalisation measures and the starting of agrarian co-operatives were greeted with boycott and blockade from the United States, which mistakenly took them to be signs of Communism. This had the effect of encouraging a large section of the Cuban bourgeoisie to emigrate to the United States – later, undesirable elements were forcibly exported there. The further radicalisation of Cuban politics, culminated in Castro's declaring the revolution to be 'socialist' following the abortive United States-backed invasion at the Bay of Pigs. Castro's initial emphasis on the support of the masses and the need for Cubans to control their own destiny were not particularly Marxist: they were a reaction to the corruption and violence that characterised the United States-backed Batista régime and Batista's middle-class allies. The manifesto of the 26 July Movement, issued in November 1956, declared:

> The 26 July Movement can be defined as guided by thinking that is democratic, nationalist, and dedicated to social justice . . . By democracy, the 26 July Movement still considers the Jeffersonian philosophy valid and fully subscribes to the formula of Lincoln of a 'government of the people, by the people, and for the people'.

In particular, Castro did not see the necessity for a party. He is quoted as saying that

> there is no revolution without a vanguard; that this vanguard is not necessarily the Marxist-Leninist Party; and that those who want to make the revolution have the right and duty to constitute themselves a vanguard, independently of these Parties.

But this is not to deny that the Cuban working class and, indeed, the Communist Party were necessary to the success of the Cuban revolution. Even at the initial assault on the Moncada barracks, there was considerable working-class support. Although the Rebel Army was composed largely of radical petty-bourgeois and peasant elements, its opposition to the ruling bourgeoisie drew strong support from the proletariat, whose general strike at the critical point in 1959 enabled Castro to take power.

In all this, the Cuban Communist Party played an inglorious role. They had actually supported the Batista régime in the 1930s; they had not participated in the armed struggle and did not come out in favour of Castro until it was clear that he would win. They were also tied to the Moscow line that the countries of Latin America and the Caribbean would have to go through a 'bourgeois democracy' in which the leading role would be taken by the national bourgeoisie: socialist measures were not on the agenda. But although the Communists looked askance at Castro, he needed the Party's organisation and trained personnel. By merging his own movement with the Communist Party, while ensuring that his supporters kept the upper hand, Castro gradually took over the Communist Party apparatus and a new Communist Party of Cuba was announced in 1965. The predominance of those with an insurrectionary background is shown by the fact that over two-thirds of the Central Committee held military titles while the eight-man Politburo had no members of the old Communist Party on it.

The guerilla origins of the revolution have left their mark on its political style. In an interview in 1968 Castro declared: 'Do you know how many real revolutionaries there were in Cuba (in 1959) at the moment of the revolution? Well, there wasn't even one per cent, not that – not even one per cent!' The result of this contempt for the revolutionary spirit of the masses is the belief that it is up to the guerilla vanguard to revolutionise Cuban society. Policies were therefore formulated by Castro and his inner circle and transmitted to the masses who were mobilised in the régime's revolutionary organisations. There was not even the façade of elections that exist in the Soviet bloc. No one was elected in Cuba as the government and Party are identical in theory as well as in practice. The spirit of the Sierra lived on in the informal system of government where ties of personal loyalty and commitment bind the leading participants to the charismatic leader. Unlike the Soviet Union or China, there have been no purges in the Cuban leadership.

The Cuban economy and society is also strongly marked by the guerilla heritage. An early crash programme to speed up industrialisation and remove the Cuban economy's dependency on sugar failed. Primary emphasis was placed on the sugar harvest and the aim of 'socialism in one island' was spearheaded by the much proclaimed goal of doubling production to achieve ten million tons by 1970. State farms were extended and even private land was rigidly controlled. Industrial production was highly centralised and by the mid-1960s Cuba had a higher proportion of State-owned property than any other country. This enabled the free provision of social services, including medical care, transport and telephones, low rent housing and 200,000 school scholarships covering all living expenses. 'The revolution cannot

Under huge portraits of socialist heroes, a demonstration of Cuba's Soviet-supplied military strength

give what it doesn't have', declared Castro, 'but what it does have it distributes in the fairest way.' The aim was to fulfil Marx's classic formula of 'from each according to his needs.'

This radical social egalitarianism went along with the declared aim of building communism at the same time as socialism. In order to build this 'new Communist man' much emphasis was put on developing Communist moral attitudes among the masses. The condemnation of the market mentality and even of money was more reminiscent of the early Marx than of subsequent Marxist practice. It was an approach which had little in common with the Marxism-Leninism to which Castro had officially declared himself committed in 1961. No doubt many Communist leaders have somehow not found the energy to plough through the whole of *Das Kapital*: Castro is the only one to have proudly professed it. Marxism-Leninism stresses historical determinism and the importance of Party organisation. What has been termed *Fidelismo* is structured around a dominant personality and derives its authority not from any class basis but from the act of rebellion itself. The role of Castro is intensely personal. But it is different from the personal rule of, say, Stalin who set aside Party and State institutions to establish his personal ascendancy. Castro was simply perpetuating the institutional vacuum which followed his guerilla victory. This lack of an institutional basis meant that Castro's authority derived from the loyalty of his followers and the support of the masses. Although there have recently been tendencies in this direction, the populist style of Castro – informal, bearded, in tatty combat jacket and boots – has meant that Cuba has not developed the kind of bureaucracy existing in the Soviet Union. As a leader, Casto is in the tradition of the Latin American *caudillo* who owes his authority to physical strength, audacity and general *machismo*.

The success of Cuba's policy of increasing sugar production to pay for industrialisation has been at best erratic. The much heralded drive for ten million tons in 1970 fell far short of its target. This was due to a combination of factors: the highly centralised and personal style of running the economy resulting in too much random intervention from above; the lack of any sort of money controls on efficiency; the diminishing returns over a long period of appeals to purely moral incentives; and finally the hit-and-run tactics typical of a guerilla movement but harmful to a national economy which requires sustained general effort rather than brief spurts of energy.

It is common among those who knew Cuba before the revolution to contrast the neon-lit high life of Havana in the 1950s with the drab and run-down city of today. Cuba is still an austere country. There are shortages of basic foodstuffs and widespread rationing. Nevertheless, the Castro régime retains widespread popular support. In contrast to Havana, the countryside is in much better shape since 1959 with new roads, irrigation schemes, and modernisation of the sugar industry. Illiteracy has been eradicated. There is considerable social mobility for the young. The more or less free social services have made a far more equal society. The irony is that this has been achieved under the leadership of Castro the supreme *caudillo* whose behaviour has much more in common with the past than with the new Communist man of the future.

Cuba has, of course, been heavily dependent on Soviet support. The Soviet bloc has supplied Cuba with most of its imports and absorbed its considerable trade deficit. The Soviet Union has also been a constant source of military aid – though the reliability of this was called into question by the sudden withdrawal of Soviet missiles from Cuba in 1962. More fundamentally, tension with the Soviet Union was increased by Castro's takeover of the Communist Party and the rejection of violent revolution by Communist Parties in such countries as Brazil, Columbia, Venezuela and Peru. In sharp distinction to the Cuban attitudes, the Soviet Union, which wished to increase diplomatic and social relations with these countries, supported the Latin American Communist Parties in attacking any strategy of armed revolution.

In the 1960s the Cubans held to the view that 'revolution was for export'. This was put into practice by Castro's right-hand man Ernesto Che

An avuncular Brezhnev poses for a photograph with Fidel Castro

Guevara and given a theory by the Frenchman Regis Debray who spent years in a Bolivian prison for his pains and is now domesticated as one of President Mitterand's closest advisers. According to Debray, the only way to overthrow the State in Latin America was 'by means of more or less slow building up, through guerilla warfare carried out in suitably chosen rural zones, of a mobile strategic force, nucleus of a people's army and of a future socialist state'. Debray considered that the subordination of the military to the political, symbolised by Mao's supremacy over Chu Teh in China, Ho Chi Minh over Giap in Vietnam, and Lenin and Trotsky's position during the Russian Civil War, was inappropriate for Latin America where the Communist Parties had not been able to take root and develop in the same way as in Russia and China. Debray's three golden rules – constant vigilance, constant mistrust, constant mobility – meant cutting off guerillas from the rest of the population, in stark contrast to Mao's approach where the peasantry was the water in which the fish swam. Thus Debray's theory involved the elevation of the military above the political in a manner quite uncharacteristic of mainstream Marxism.

Debray's theory was also premised upon the view that the Cuban experience could be repeated. But there is much evidence that the Cuban revolution was highly specific and therefore unrepeatable. The aim of the Cuban revolution was, at its beginning, a democratic reformist government; the peasants had already largely been proletarianised by large mechanised capitalist farms; there was an absence of intervention by the United States; and finally, even the bourgeoisie was disaffected with the Batista régime. The general result of this lack of political analysis in theories such as Debray's is a combination of a Hispanic revolutionary ethic with an American concentration on the technical details of guerilla war which are only linked by a military romanticism. This outlook has affinities with recent urban terrorist movements in Western Europe – the Baader-Meinhof group in Germany and the Red Brigades in Italy.

Indeed, throughout Latin America, Marxism has been mainly associated with unsuccessful guerilla movements. Both the Sino-Soviet split and the antipathy of Castro to the orthodox Communist Parties meant the fragmentation of the Marxist movement. Moscow was loath to give any substantial support to the Communist Parties of Latin America which it regarded as being firmly in the Western sphere of influence. During the 1970s, guerilla movements such as the Tupamaros in Uruguay and the Monteneros in Argentina flourished briefly in the more developed South and East but succumbed eventually to brutal government repression. The marriage of peasant nationalism and Marxism that has been so powerful in Asia failed to take place in Latin America.

Regis Debray, former theoretician to Che Guevara and Latin American guerrillas, now adviser to President Mitterand

Following the death of Guevara in the Bolivian jungle in 1968, Cuba has tended to play down the export of revolution and thereby forge closer links with Moscow. In spite of giving aid and succour to independence movements in Angola, Cuba has tried, with some success, to renew relations with the United States over the last five years. Recently, however, the United States has put Cuba back into cold war quarantine, blaming Cuba for the success of the Sandinista guerillas in Nicaragua and the civil war in El Salvador. The guerilla movements in Central America have enough popular support not to need to rely on Cuba and the attitude of the United States is likely to make Cuban dependence on the Soviet Union even more pronounced. In spite of its links with Cuba, it does not follow that the Soviet Union is keen on the export of revolution. The programme of world revolution belonging to the days of Lenin and the Comintern is long outmoded. For the very successes of Communism worldwide have weakened the Russian position. At least in the time of Stalin, the Communist movement had its undisputed centre in Moscow. Now there is dissension between Communist Parties which are a source of competition, challenge Moscow's line, and occasionally even make war on each other. The fostering of Communist revolution in China has resulted in creating the Soviet Union's most bitter enemy. Now the Soviet Union has to station forty-five divisions on the long border adjoining the world's most populous nation.

Although the Soviet Union is cautious in its assistance to revolutionary movements it is in the Third World that Marxism is likely to prove most effective in changing the world in the near future. For many developing countries have looked to the Soviet experience as the most striking model available for rapid development. In such countries, the whole concept of planning and of a single vanguard party mobilising all human resources for rapid social change are very attractive. Liberation and emancipation have been watchwords of Marxism from the Young Marx onwards and have a natural resonance in the ears of oppressed peoples. The political traditions of the West, by contrast, are seen as belonging to former colonisers and present exploiters, and ineffective as a framework for development. It is no coincidence that three countries in Africa which have the best claim to be taking Marxism seriously – Angola, Mozambique and Guinea-Bissau – are all ex-Portuguese colonies. The MPLA in Angola and FRELIMO in Mozambique were both substantially aided by the Soviet Union, including – in Angola – the presence of 20,000 Cuban troops. The availability of Soviet aid, lengthy guerilla struggles, the mass exodus of the whites and extreme poverty in both countries have facilitated the emergence of Spartan one-party states hoping to develop through an austerely self-reliant form of Marxism. For Marxism has no real rival as an ideology of modernisation.

A young Angolan looks over a bookshop with Communist literature and portraits of Che Guevara and Fidel Castro

The experience of the three countries we have been considering in detail has brought something new into the Marxist tradition and pushed it further away from Marx himself. This experience has also posed new problems. Firstly, what happens after the death of charismatic leaders? By and large, the democratic systems of the West have been successful in shelving away the Men of Providence once they have outlived their usefulness – Churchill being perhaps the most obvious case. A collectivist ideology, on the other hand, finds the notion of an individual leader difficult to deal with in any case. Marxism gives little formal recognition to the role of the individual, and the death of the leader has often left an institutional vacuum – as in the case of both Mao and Tito. Secondly, all three countries show a tension between their Marxism and an emergent nationalism. Marxism is an international doctrine which relies on a class solidarity that transcends national boundaries. The occurrence of deep divisions and even war between Marxist states poses obvious problems. Thirdly, there is the sense of unfinished revolution. Mao was explicit about this and tried to bring about a state of more or less permanent revolution. Cuba considers itself to be part of a continuing world revolution. But there comes a point where revolutionary fervour and ideals are forced to compromise and the spirit of the revolution is in danger of being drowned in a swamp of bureaucracy. Since the original aims were so grandiose, disillusion can be all the more swift and destructive.

6

MARX COMES HOME

> The dispute over the reality or non-reality of thinking
> that is isolated from practice is a purely scholastic
> question.
>
> Karl Marx

The most diverse forms of Marxism have successfully spread across the world: the one area where Marxism has failed to make comparable progress is in its birthplace in the Western industrial nations. Immediately after the Paris Commune, Marx wrote:

> The battle must break out again and in ever-growing dimensions, and there can be no doubt as to who will be the victor in the end – the appropriating few or the immense working majority. The French working class is only the vanguard of the modern proletariat.

And in his last published work Marx spoke of the possibility of the Russian revolution being 'a signal for proletarian revolution in the West, so that both complement each other'. Marx's view of history implied that the advanced capitalist countries – Germany, France, Britain, the United States – were also the ripest for socialism. For modern capitalism had provided the technology that made socialism possible. It had provided a capitalist class who owned the factories, and it had also provided the industrial working class, the proletariat. They owned nothing except their labour which they were obliged to sell to the capitalists. Marx taught that the contradictions of capitalism, the crises of over-production and slump, the inevitable class conflict between the capitalists and the proletariat, would only be resolved by a socialist revolution. And he often talked as though it was just around the corner and imminent. But the fact is, of course, that it is precisely these countries where there was no revolution of the sort Marx so confidently predicted. Instead, the socialist revolution which he wanted and of which he dreamed and to which he devoted his entire life, came to quite another sort of country, to Russia – a backward country with no advanced technology, a country with a fairly small capitalist class, and a correspondingly small industrial proletariat. And in the two-thirds of a century since the Russian Revolution, the fulfilment of Marx's prediction has had to wait. A Marxist revolution is possible, indeed is likely in precisely those countries which do *not* possess an advanced technological base, which do *not* have a well-developed capitalist class and where there is *not* a large industrial army of wage earners, a modern proletariat. As Trotsky remarked wistfully after 1917, history seemed to be unravelling its skein in the wrong direction – East to West rather than West to East.

It is nevertheless a striking paradox that the very fact that Marxism has not triumphed in the West means that it has not been turned into an official ideology and is thus the object of serious study unimpeded by governmental controls. It is precisely in Western Europe and America – the capitalist countries – that Marx is studied most carefully. Indeed, it is fair to say that there are more real Marxists in the West than in many of the so-called 'Marxist' countries. In the West, more than anywhere else, Marxism has had great difficulty in coming to terms with its own history. Over the last two decades in particular, stridently different interpretations of Marx have been developed in the capitalist countries. The two main problems confronting these interpretations have been the non-occurrence of revolution in the West and the long shadow that Stalinism has cast on the rest of European Marxism. The two are, of course, linked.

The Bolshevik revolution could not but have a profound effect on international Marxism. Before the First World War, Western Europe was the centre of Marxism with large and well-organised Marxist parties, particularly in Germany, grouped together in the Second International. As early as 1914, however, Lenin had envisaged the founding of another International to replace the Second International with whose leaders and policies he had become utterly disillusioned. The Second International had been infected, so he thought, by opportunists corrupted by the fruits of imperialism. This could only be avoided in the future by strong central control. In other words, the organisation of the new International would have to be modelled on that of the Russian Bolshevik Party. Before the October Revolution, few Marxists in the West had much sympathy for, or interest in, Leninist organisational principles. But its victory in Russia naturally gave Leninism enormous prestige as a model – in spite of the evidently different social and economic conditions in most of Western Europe.

Lenin's plans soon came to fruition. A Third or Communist International was formed in Moscow in the spring of 1919. Those parties adhering to the Comintern (as it came to be known) were at first rather varied. There were parties, such as the Hungarian, formed by returning prisoners of war who had learnt all about Bolshevism from their enforced stay in Russia; there were left-wing splinter groups who had broken off from mainstream socialism, such as the German Spartacists; and there were socialist parties who

Street fighting in Berlin in 1918/19. The failure of the revolution in Germany meant the isolation of the Soviet Union and paved the way for Stalinism

adhered *en bloc* of whom the most important was the Italian. There were even a few anarchists, curiously united with the Bolsheviks in their common hatred of socialist 'betrayal'.

By the next year, however, the atmosphere had changed. Lenin had decided finally to split the European labour movement and when the delegates assembled in 1920 they found that their membership of the Comintern was to be conditional on acceptance of the famous twenty-one points. In sum, these points declared that Communists should strive systematically to exclude centrists and reformists from all positions of influence in the labour movement and replace them with reliable Party members; Communist Parties should create underground organisations; the decisions of national organisations could be overruled by the Executive Committee of the Comintern; and, most significantly, the structure of the nascent Communist Parties should be completely Bolshevised: 'In the present phase of acute civil war, a Communist Party will only be able to do its duty provided it is organised with the highest possible degree of centralisation and keeps iron discipline; the central committee, backed by the confidence of the members, must be vested with complete power, authority, and the most far-reaching qualifications.'

The long-term consequences of these measures were two-fold. Firstly

Moscow emerged as the clear leader of international Communism, replacing Paris as the centre of revolution. The inevitable prestige of revolutionary success was confirmed by the choice of Moscow as the seat of the Comintern and the nomination to its Presidency of Zinoviev, a powerful orator whose capacity for double-dealing was matched only by his subservience to Lenin. Secondly, factionalism became inherent in the Communist Parties. Of course, all parties have factional divisions, which tend to be united in times of success and exacerbated in the face of failure. But these divisions reached an extraordinary intensity in the Communist Parties. This was due to their double illusion of expecting a revolution to occur in the near future and expecting it to be initiated by the organised activity of a small vanguard. When these expectations failed to materialise, the only explanation was that there had been a betrayal by a specified person or persons. Just as the heretic is a more insidious opponent than the outright unbeliever, so Communists looked for individual scapegoats within their own ranks. (The prime model here, of course, was the purging by Stalin himself of all his old Bolshevik comrades.) The European Communists should have asked, in a properly Marxist fashion, whether the economic and social conditions were ripe for revolution. A clear-sighted answer to such a question might, of course, have deprived the Communist Parties of their *raison d'être*. Instead, aided and abetted by Moscow, they found the (very un-Marxist) explanation for their failure in the existence in their ranks of individual traitors. Continual purges were the only sustenance that could keep their revolutionary hopes alive.

It has often been thought that the Comintern was simply an instrument of Soviet foreign policy. This was largely true after 1934 with the emergence in Russia of the full Stalinist system and the rise to power of Hitler in Germany. But initially world revolution was genuinely on the agenda. It was an era of boundless hope among the Russians. A Soviet Republic, backed by demobilised soldiers, had been proclaimed in Hungary in 1918 led by the cruel and hysterical Bela Kun together with George Lukacs, one of the foremost Marxist theoreticians of the century, as People's Commissar for Education. The Hungarian experiment was short-lived, brought down by its own blunders and extremism.

More serious was the failure to unseat the very unrevolutionary socialist government that came to power in Germany immediately after defeat in the war. In Berlin, the uprising led by the Spartacists was swiftly overcome by government troops. The bumbling approach of the revolutionaries is well conveyed by the story that at the height of the disturbances the leaders of the insurrection sent a group of workers to take over the Ministry of War – one of the few offices that had not been evacuated by the Govern-

Rosa Luxemburg, the most gifted of the Marxist leaders in Germany, photographed about five years before her murder in the 1918 uprising

ment. The leader of the group went into the building and was told by the officers in charge that his warrant, although signed by the revolutionary leaders, lacked an authoritative stamp. The man, a worker who had never been in politics before, went to fetch the stamp but changed his mind and instead returned home to spend the rest of the day in bed. The most tragic upshot of the rising was the murder of Rosa Luxemburg. A brief Soviet Republic was quickly and brutally suppressed by the army. The forces of the right gained in strength and the young Communist Party was decimated. It boded ill, too, for the fate of the Russian revolution the success of which the Bolsheviks has always said would depend on revolution in Europe.

But the German failures were repeated elsewhere. Western Europe was not Russia and the attempts of the new Communist Parties to imitate the Bolsheviks in going it alone proved disastrous. In 1921 the Comintern authorities decided to pursue a policy of a United Front, which meant co-operation with socialist parties in the struggle for common aims such as better wages and working conditions. The fact that it was often difficult to see the difference between this and reformism or opportunism involved the need for even closer control from Moscow. But politics in Moscow at this time was itself subject to factionalism. The struggle between Stalin and Trotsky was about to reach its height in Russia. Another ill-planned rising in Germany in 1923 had been supported by Trotsky who was much more enthusiastic about the international dimensions of Communism than was Stalin. The failure of the rising was used as a pretext for getting rid of his friends in the German leadership. As Trotsky began to lose out inside Russia, his supporters were removed from the leadership of the national parties. Although the Trotskyists were often revolutionary romantics, at least they had opinions of their own: those who replaced them were largely yes-men.

The final victory of Stalin in Russia coincided with the most disastrous period of Comintern policy in Europe. In 1929 wild revolutionary hopes alternating with despair were being produced by the depression. The extremism of Stalin's forced collectivisation of Russian agriculture was transferred to the European scene. Molotov took charge of the Comintern and 'class against class' was the new slogan. Socialists of all hues were anathematised as lackeys of the bourgeoisie and 'social fascists'. As the power of the Nazis grew, Communists fought socialists in the streets of Germany – only to meet a few years later in Nazi concentration camps. By the time there was a change of line in 1934 and it was realised that socialism was not, after all, the main enemy, it was far too late and Hitler was firmly in power. In keeping with the growing isolation and nationalism of the Soviet Union, the Communist Parties adopted a nationalist stance. The notion of world revolution was, said Stalin, 'a tragi-comical misunderstanding'. The personality cult of Stalin, too, was transferred to the other Parties and leaders such as Thorez in France and Pollitt in Britain were treated to similar adulation. The abrupt change of party line in 1934 with the resumption of a United Front against Fascism and again in 1939 following the Nazi-Soviet pact revealed the adherents of the Comintern to be mere puppets and the Comintern itself to be an instrument of Soviet power.

This sorry state of affairs was seen at its clearest in the Spanish Civil War, the one place where the Comintern was still to play a significant (and tragic) role. The Spanish Communists, aided by Russian arms and Russian commissars, gradually gained control of the Spanish left. Forty thousand idealists flocked to the International Brigade to combat Franco. But the Soviet Union did not wish to antagonise the British and French governments. The Communists soon became the refuge of the propertied middle classes *against* the strong non-Communist revolutionary movement that had grown up in Catalonia. And it was the Communists who eventually crushed the Trotskyist and Anarchist-led proletariat of Barcelona more effectively than any Fascists.

With the outbreak of the Second World War the Comintern became little more than an embarrassment. It had, in any case, for long been a dead letter and was disbanded in 1943. The consequences of the Party line for the Soviet Union were at least debatable: for the rest of Europe (and beyond) it was an undeniable disaster.

The legacy of the Comintern has recently begun to weigh less heavily on the European Communist Parties. With the public exposure of Stalin's feet of clay and the subsequent Sino-Soviet dispute, Moscow's grip on the Communist Parties lessened. In Italy and France, the leading role played by the Communists in the Resistance enabled them to become, for the first time, organisations which commanded the support of the majority of the working class. With the emergence into legality of the Spanish Communist Party, following the death of Franco, the concept of Eurocommunism was born.

The pacesetter in holding Moscow at arm's length and opting for the parliamentary road to socialism is the Italian Communist Party. In the post-Stalin era of Western European Communism the central figure was the Italian Communist leader Palmiro Togliatti. Togliatti had always maintained a fairly independent line, but the Krushchev speech of 1956 gave him the opportunity of broadening his position by declaring, firstly, that the mere criticism of Stalin as a person was too superficial an approach to the phenomenon of Stalinism; secondly, that the construction of socialism was possible in a multi-party state; and thirdly that the whole Communist

Palmiro Togliatti, the Italian Communist leader who distanced the Italian Communist Party from Moscow

movement had become a polycentral system in which Moscow no longer held the unique place. In line with these views, Togliatti's Yalta Memorandum of 1964, composed just before his death as a kind of political testament, took issue with the positions taken up by the Chinese Communist Party but equally opposed their formal condemnation by the Soviet Union. Togliatti claimed that 'any proposal to create once again a centralised international organisation' was unacceptable, and stated firmly:

We always start from the idea that Socialism is the régime in which there is the widest freedom for the workers, that they in fact participate in an organised manner in the direction of the entire social life. Therefore, we greet all positions of principle and all facts showing us that this is the reality in all the Socialist countries and not only in the Soviet Union. On the other hand, events that sometimes disclose the contrary to us damage the entire movement.

Togliatti's ideas were given wide currency by the Communist Party of Italy in recent years, and have led to the famous 'historic compromise' in which the Party, in the hope of extending its own power base, has been willing to give qualified support to parties whose basic orientation is not socialist.

Italy not only has the largest Communist Party in the West with nearly two million members: it also possesses the legacy of the most important of Western Marxists, Antonio Gramsci, with which to bolster its novel policies. A hunchback born in Sardinia in 1896 to middle-class parents fallen on hard times, Gramsci turned early to journalism. During the two 'red years' of 1919–20, he was the main inspiration behind the movement to establish workers' control of the factories in Turin. From 1921 to 1926, after the foundation of the Italian Communist Party, Gramsci, as one of its leaders and a close friend of Togliatti, was involved in formulating its policies and conducting negotiations with the Comintern. Finally, he fell a victim to the Fascists in 1926 and languished in one of Mussolini's prisons until his death in 1937. It was here that he produced his major theoretical work – the *Prison Notebooks*.

Gramsci strongly modified the ideas of both Marx and Lenin. He saw Marx as having greatly underestimated the resilience of capitalist society. In Marx's dichotomy of economic base and political and ideological super-structure, Gramsci considered that too little attention had been paid to the latter and he emphasised the importance of ideas and culture in general in the political process. One of the main reasons why revolution had failed in the West was that the mass of the people were not convinced of the value of socialism and still clung to capitalist versions of liberty, equality and democracy. Not until the power of bourgeois ideology had been broken could Marxism become attractive to the large numbers of people. Thus one of the major tasks of Communists (and an important revolutionary activity in itself) was to try to establish a kind of socialist counter-culture, an alternative vision of the world to the (at present) seemingly inevitable and natural attitudes of capitalism. Only then could the proletariat gain hegemony (a favourite term of Gramsci) or leadership over all the forces in society that opposed capitalism.

Antonio Gramsci, probably the most original Marxist thinker of the twentieth century

Nor, according to Gramsci, had Lenin provided a satisfactory revolutionary programme for the West. The strategy of frontal assault may have been successful in Russia where the State was a wobbly autocratic structure imposed on a society with no solid middle-class institutions. But it would not do for Western Europe where political authority was much more firmly supported by society. In a powerful metaphor, Gramsci wrote:

> In Russia the State was everything, civil society was primordial and gelatinous; in the West, there was a proper relationship between State and civil society, and when the State trembled a sturdy structure of civil society was at once revealed. The State was only an outer ditch, behind which there stood a powerful system of fortresses and earthworks.

In other words, one of the major tasks confronting contemporary Marxists was to undermine the political concepts of capitalist society as a necessary preliminary to attempting any revolution.

The ideas of Gramsci are often rather obscure as they were couched in veiled language to escape the prison censorship. But they have been appropriated by the Italian Communist Party as a justification of their 'third way' between the mild reforms of social democracy and the uncompromisingly revolutionary stance of Leninism. The Italian Communists have taken issue with Moscow over Poland, where they strongly supported Solidarity, and over Afghanistan. The Party General Secretary Enrico Berlinguer claimed that the Soviet Union had endangered world peace by invading Afghanistan since 'a violation of sovereignty made in the name of one cause stimulates a violation in the name of a contrary cause'. The Communists do not want to remove Italy from NATO and are as enthusiastic as any other party for law and order in the face of Red Brigade terrorism. This independence and moderation has gained the Communist Party widespread popularity in Italy and it draws strength and support from all sections of society. It has also acquired a good reputation in local government – in Bologna, for instance, where the Red Flag has been flying over the Town Hall ever since the end of the war. The Communists have the reputation here – and elsewhere – of being the 'clean' party as opposed to the Christian Democrats whose corruption is notorious. Nevertheless, the Communists are unlikely to attain power in central government for the foreseeable future. Support for them has levelled off at about a third of the electorate; their natural allies, the Socialists, have moved strongly to the right lately; tacit support in the past for the Christian Democrats has not proved popular electorally; and the Party itself is more comfortable in opposition than having directly to confront the chaotic problems of Italy's economy and society.

The French and Spanish Communist Parties have, in the 1970s, followed the Italian lead. Formerly quite the model of Third International propriety, the French Party decided to abandon the Soviet model of socialism as its goal, insisted on a socialism 'in French colours' and formed an electoral alliance and common programme with the Socialist Party. In 1976, the French Communist Party even decided to drop the aim of 'dictatorship of the proletariat' from its programme. However, the French Party showed none of the flexibility of their Italian comrades in trying to broaden the base of their support. The Eurocommunist attitudes were never really embraced by the Party. The principal beneficiaries of the rise of the left in France have been the Socialists, culminating in the election of Mitterand as President in May 1981. The Communist share of the vote dropped dramatically and, in spite of having four ministers in the government, the Party is undoubtedly looking for an occasion to split with the Socialists. They are unhappy in the role of junior partners and need to rebuild their appeal as the major party of the left. With their support for Soviet policy over Afghanistan and Poland, they are going to find this difficult.

To date, the most outspoken proponent of Eurocommunism has been the Spanish Communist Party. This is natural, as the Spanish Party is anxious to defend and gain full advantage from Spain's new and fragile democracy after decades of persecution under Franco. Its former General Secretary Santiago Carillo, in his controversial book *Eurocommunism and the State*, lays stress on the achievement and extension of democratic liberties and human rights and sees the gaining of an electoral mandate as an essential step in the struggle to transform capitalism. In a passage which obviously refers to the Soviet Union, Carillo goes as far as to say:

> In actual fact the lack of democratic 'credibility' of us communists among certain sections of the population in our countries is associated – rather than with our own activity and policy – with the fact that in countries where capital ownership has disappeared, the dictatorship of the proletariat has been implanted, with a one-party system, as a general rule, and has undergone serious bureaucratic distortions and even very grave processes of degeneration.

At its 1978 Congress, the Party even decided, in spite of strident opposition from Moscow, to abandon any specific reference to Leninism in its self-definition.

In general, the Communist Parties of Western Europe face colossal problems. The Russian legacy makes it difficult for them to operate in parliamentary democracies. Decades of subservience to Moscow have created suspicions about how far they have the interests of their fellow-citizens at heart. In spite of operating in liberal democracies, their inner-party democ-

Night scene from the May 1968 riots in Paris

racy is still of the centralist type inherited from Lenin with all the hierarchy and secrecy that alienates friend as well as foe. Immediately after the war, there was a chance of radical change among the Communist Parties. They participated not only in parliament but actually in government in Italy, France, Belgium, Luxembourg, Austria, Norway, Denmark, Finland and Iceland. But the Cold War brought an abrupt halt to this kind of collaboration. Although the era of détente has done much to bring the Communists back into national life, it is only too easy (as the French Communist Party has recently shown) for the Communist Party to return to being a kind of complete sub-culture cut off from, and opposed to, the rest of society. It is this mentality which gives rise to the impression that Parties who have been talking for decades of revolution are surprisingly reluctant to assume power. The classic instance is the extremely passive role played by the French Communist Party during the troubles of May 1968. In marked contrast to the Trotskyists and the anarchists, the main object for the Communists seemed to be to get a hefty wage rise for their members and return to the *status quo* as soon as possible. This preference for the role of opposition is no doubt due in part to the fear of provoking a backlash: the folk memory of the French Left extends back to the bloody suppression of the Commune. There is also the fear that sharing power with 'bourgeois' parties would compromise them in the eyes of their own working-class supporters. Finally, any large organised Marxist party in a capitalist country fits too easily into the existing society. Its leaders become bureaucrats. They have spent a lifetime as professional revolutionaries without a revolution, often not even in search of a revolution. Thus the biggest obstacle to a Marxist revolution is often the Party itself.

Nor have the Communist Parties of the West any coherent strategy in terms of which to work out long term policies. Around 1960, there emerged the notion of 'state monopoly capitalism' which asserted that the economies of the West were undergoing increased domination by monopolies which had taken control of the State and manipulated it for their own benefit. This rather vague notion implied the disappearance of the capitalists-versus-the-proletariat and its replacement by the monopolies-versus-the-people and enabled the Communists to propose themselves as potential leaders of virtually the whole citizenry who, if elected, would use state power to expropriate the monopolies. The aim of such a strategy was to build a coalition of the discontented that would be as broad as possible. Politically, the policies that corresponded to this economic analysis were: the idea that there would be a peaceful transition to socialism through parliament; the necessity for alliance with other parties; and the acceptance of the right of other parties to exist even in a Communist-dominated government. How far these changes are simply opportunistic, is of course, difficult to say. A crucial question is whether a Communist government, if elected, would be willing to submit itself to the possibility of defeat at the next scheduled elections. The fact that the Communists view this as a false problem (since they cannot contemplate losing majority support) does not inspire confidence. Still trapped between the legacy of Lenin and the temptations of bourgeois democracy, the Communist Parties have yet to discover for themselves a convincing role in the West.

What, then, of the Trotskyist parties, whose hatred of Moscow equals that of any capitalist? At the Twentieth Congress of the Communist Party of the Soviet Union in 1956 Krushchev declared that Stalin had 'sanctioned in the name of the Central Committee of the All-Union Communist Party (Bolsheviks) the most brutal violation of socialist legality, torture and oppression which led to the slander and self-accusation of innocent people'. This denunciation sent a shock around the Marxist world that affected more than the official Communist Parties. It gave a great boost to the Trotskyists who were able to say: we told you so. For Trotskyism is the one organised branch of revolutionary Marxism that can claim descent from Marx through Lenin and has yet remained untainted by the phenomenon of Stalinism. Trotsky himself was naturally concerned to justify the Bolshevik revolution in which he had played such a prominent part. The decade between his exile from the Soviet Union in 1929 and his murder at Stalin's behest in Mexico in 1940 gave Trotsky ample time to meditate on what had gone wrong.

Unlike Lenin, who had implied in *State and Revolution* that the problem could be overcome by political and administrative measures, Trotsky saw bureaucracy as rooted in Russia's social and historical circumstances. It was the product of backwardness. In *The Revolution Betrayed* – his major work on the subject, written in 1936 – he gave this account of Soviet bureaucracy:

> The basis of bureaucratic rule is the poverty of society in objects of consumption with the resulting struggle of each against all. When there are enough goods in the store the purchasers can come whenever they want to. When there are little goods the purchasers are compelled to stand in line. When the lines are very long, it is necessary to appoint a policeman to keep order. Such is the starting point of the power of Soviet bureaucracy.

The consequent problem however, of how the rise of a bureaucracy in a backward country like Russia could be avoided and thus whether 1917 itself was a mistake was never adequately answered by Trotsky.

Trotsky was quite clear that the Soviet Union was not just another form of capitalism and that the bureaucracy was not therefore a ruling class:

> The bureaucracy has neither stocks nor bonds. It is recruited, supplemented and renewed in the manner of an administrative hierarchy independent of any property relations of its own. The individual cannot transmit to his heirs his rights in the exploitation of the State apparatus. The bureaucracy enjoys its privileges under the form of the abuse of power.

Since the Soviet Union already enjoyed socialist forms of ownership, the Soviet bureaucracy was merely a parasite, in Trotsky's words, 'a monstrous and continually growing social distortion which in turn becomes the source of malignant growths in society'. The optimistic conclusion was that in the Soviet Union, as distinct from the capitalist West, a merely political revolution was needed to get rid of the bureaucracy: state ownership had already laid the economic basis for socialism.

In 1934 Trotsky founded the Fourth International in opposition to Stalin's Third International or Comintern, and his followers are to be found all over the world. They are in fact strongly committed to internationalism and scorn Stalin's idea of socialism in one country. The Stalinist ice-pick buried in his skull in 1940 turned Trotsky into a martyr: Trotsky represents the conscience of the revolution and Trotskyism remains attractive to all revolutionaries who wish to preserve the ideals of the Bolshevik revolution. Its main theme is still the revolutionary potential of the working class in the West. Since Trotskyism has been so unsuccessful that it has never been

The conscience of the revolution: Trotsky as Commissar for War, 1924

saddled with the responsibility of exercising real power, its hands have not thereby been dirtied. Its outright rejection of any form of 'bourgeois' democracy has preserved it from any compromise in that direction. But equally, this purity of doctrine has bred extreme sectarianism: in Britain, as elsewhere, the catalogue of Trotskyist groups, often violently opposed to one another is bewildering, and the series of initials, IMG, SWP, RCT etc. etc. seemingly endless. The lack of any substantial support among the very proletariat in which they put their trust has resulted in dozens of Trotskyist 'vanguards' with no one to follow them. Recently, and particularly in

Britain, some Trotskyists have taken to 'entryism': despairing of the efficacy of their own small groups, they have infiltrated larger organisations such as the Labour Party in the hope of pushing them in a more revolutionary direction. Constant prediction of economic catastrophes in the West has become with time little more than an incantation. The dedication and evident sincerity of many of their members meet with little response. Conservative in its constant appeal to the theories that Marx and Lenin evolved in far other contexts, Trotskyism is the version of Marxism at the furthest remove from contemporary reality.

The demise of Stalinism and the Soviet invasion of Hungary in 1956 brought about the upsurge of a very different kind of Marxism that came to be known as the New Left. It was more defined by what it rejected than by what it affirmed. The New Left was opposed both to the shallow materialist capitalism of the West and to the authoritarian Leninist tradition both in its Stalinist and in its Trotskyist forms. Rejecting both East and West, they tended to look to the Third World for their heroes. The product of affluence more than poverty, the New Left was a revolt against the kind of society produced by the long post-war capitalist boom, and it disappeared with the end of that boom in the early 1970s. Its apogee was reached in the events of May 1968 in Paris. These events were a strange mixture: there was an echo of the heroic, romantic age of 1848. Even the language, the symbolic actions of the revolutionaries – most of whom were students – had a dated air of 1848 about them. The riot of graffiti and slogans such as *l'imagination au pouvoir* revealed the Utopian aspects of the revolt. Under the threat of military intervention and with the calling of a general election, the upheaval subsided as quickly as it had arisen. Of course, it was not a revolutionary situation. The French Communist Party kept well in the background and French capitalism emerged unharmed at the end of it.

The New Left was by nature and inclination amorphous. Nevertheless, three main themes can be discerned. Firstly, there was the wholesale rejection of the existing order of things. The whole of contemporary society was corrupt and therefore the revolution must be worldwide and total. Thus any attempt at reform was really a plot to preserve the existing powers. Secondly, there was distrust of the working class of Western industrial countries who has been irredeemably infected by the system. Thirdly, and as a consequence, liberation had to come from those supposedly outside the system whether students and other minority groups in the West or from the Third World where the New Left found its chief exemplars. As will be readily gleaned from these three characteristics, the New Left was often more a state of mind than a theory of society. It had more in common with anarchism and with the extreme versions of Maoism that filtered through to the West at the time of the Cultural Revolution than with mainstream Marxism. The only area where some New Left thinkers linked up with the main socialist tradition was in their advocacy of workers' control of production. This idea was not Marxist in origin: it had been advocated in the nineteenth century on the Continent by anarchists such as Proudhon and Bakunin and in England by the Guild Socialists. But it has surfaced from time to time within Marxism, advocated by those who, disillusioned with state ownership whether in the East or the West, have seen that nationalisation of industry would not of itself solve any major problem and look for a form of collectivism without exploitation.

Although the New Left was not given to coherent exposition, the thinker who most nearly represented their outlook was Herbert Marcuse. It was his work *One-Dimensional Man* which became the Bible of the revolutionaries of 1968. Of German origin, Marcuse had settled in the United States and his views were formed by his experience of American society. *One-Dimensional Man* marked a fundamental change in the traditional Marxist perspective. Although Marcuse agreed that capitalists and proletarians were still the basic classes in industrial society,

> The capitalist development has altered the structure and function of these two classes in such a way that they no longer appear to be agents of historical transformation. An overriding interest in the preservation and improvement of the institutional status quo unites the former antagonists in the most advanced areas of contemporary society.

And the same was true of Communist societies such as the Soviet Union. Moreover, Marcuse starkly declared that advanced industrial societies, whether in the West or in the East, were totalitarian:

> For 'totalitarian' is not only a terroristic political co-ordination of society, but also a non-terroristic economic-technical co-ordination which operates through the manipulation of needs by vested interests. It thus precludes the emergence of an effective opposition against the whole. Not only a specific form of government or party rule makes for totalitarianism, but also a specific system of production and distribution which may well be compatible with a 'pluralism' of parties, newspapers, 'countervailing powers', etc.

This totalitarianism was all the more secure as it seemed to have no conscious economic or political direction. Technological society appeared to have satisfied men's needs and thus offered no room for protest. Marcuse attempted to distinguish between true and false needs. But what men's real needs were could not be determined at present, for

Herbert Marcuse whose book *One-Dimensional Man* was one of the main inspirations behind the New Left of the late 1960s and early 1970s

in the last analysis, the question of what are true and false needs must be answered by the individuals themselves, but only in the last analysis: that is, if and when they're free to give their own answer.

This obviously left unresolved the question of how society which totally controlled the consciousness of its members could possibly change; and the bulk of *One-Dimensional Man* was devoted to demonstrating the all-pervasive nature of this control. In the realm of art, for example, the material advances of society had produced 'a harmonising pluralism where the most contradictory works and truths peacefully coexist in indifference'. In sexual matters, too, an 'institutionalised desublimation' had taken place:

> Sex is integrated into work and public relations and thus is made more susceptible to (controlled) satisfaction. Technical progress and more comfortable living permit the systematic inclusion of libidinal components into the realm of commodity production and exchange.

Even language itself was progressively becoming a closed system which precluded even linguistic expression of opposition.

In the face of such a society, what hope was there for change? Marcuse stated at the beginning of his work that he vacillated between two contradictory hypotheses. The first was that advanced industrial society was capable of containing qualitative change for the foreseeable future; and the second that forces and tendencies existed which might break this containment and explode society. Throughout *One-Dimensional Man* the emphasis was on the first tendency. The possibility that the second tendency might come to the fore was only raised very briefly at the end of the book. This tendency would have to be based on those who existed outside the 'democratic process' – 'the substratum of the outcasts and outsiders, the exploited and persecuted of other races and other colours, the unemployed and the unemployable.' But for Marcuse, this could only be an 'accident':

> The chance is that the historical extremes may meet again: the most advanced consciousness of humanity, and its most exploited force. It is nothing but a chance. The critical theory of society possesses no concepts which could bridge the gap between the present and its future: holding no promise and showing no success, it remains negative.

In general, the ideas of the New Left can be seen as a rejection of many major Marxist themes from Marx himself onwards. Marx was emphatic that it was the working class who would revolutionise society: it was the very workings of the capitalist economy that would produce its own gravediggers in the shape of the proletariat. The New Left despaired of the working class who had been too well integrated into 'the system'. They therefore looked to fringe minority groups to oppose this system. Here they had more in common with the anarchist tradition which turned to those outside society as the only ones who really did have nothing to lose and would therefore be willing to throw the bombs. Again, Marx was enormously enthusiastic about modern technology. One of the greatest achievements of capitalism, in his eyes, had been to increase the productive forces with the growth of machinery, expertise and specialisation. Of course, these advances were currently used in the service of capitalist interests, but Marx clearly saw socialism as the inheritor of capitalist science and technology – the very progress of which had made socialism possible. The New Left, on the other hand, hated modern technology and opposed any authority derived from expertise and specialisation. Finally, Marx was a Eurocentric thinker who saw the rest of the world as following in Europe's wake. The New Left, having despaired of advanced capitalism tended to look to the Third World for their models of revolution with Guevara or Mao as their heroes rather than anyone nearer home.

For a brief period, the New Left was as successful in America, Britain and Germany as elsewhere. In fact, it was the one ephemeral and much mutated form of Marxism to have made any impact on the Anglo-Saxon world. Indeed, it is one of the major weaknesses of contemporary Marxism that it has so little support in the original heartland of capitalism. In West Germany, the absence of any resistance movement such as existed in France and Italy and hostility to the officially Marxist East Germany meant that the pre-war Communist tradition was virtually eliminated. Although the German Communist Party was permitted again in 1971, its members are still prevented from holding public office or employment – even as teachers in some provinces. The 'German economic miracle' (which was anything but a miracle, and has simpler explanations – the strength of German technical culture, massive investment from abroad and from the banking system, influx of labour, Germany's traditional place in centre of Europe, her size, etc.) and the great rise in standards of living, may have slowed, but German capitalism is still strong. There is a sincere anti-capitalist student movement, but it is not solidly based in the proletariat – hence the turn to extremism by such as the Baader-Meinhof group.

In Britain, as the first industrialised country, a mature form of socialism was already well under way before Marx's name became known after 1880. In the Independent Labour Party and later in the Labour Party, it was a form of socialism that drew much inspiration from non-conformist religion and so was hostile to what appeared to be the dogmatic and jejune materialism of Marxism. The relative success of the Labour Party in gaining concessions for the working class made Marxism seem too extreme and intolerant

VOTE FOR

Home Rule.

Democratic
Government.

Justice to Labour

No Monopoly.

No Landlordism

Temperance
Reform.

Healthy Homes.

Fair Rents.

Eight-Hour Day.

Work for the
Unemployed.

KEIR HARDIE.

Printed and Published by F. W. Scr se & Co, [L.S.C], 151, Barking Road, Canning Town, London, E.

An election poster of the early Labour leader Keir Hardie, showing a
number of slogans with a moral and social slant foreign to Marxism

an attitude. The British Communist Party was the only European Communist Party not to have been formed as a result of a split from the majority
Social Democratic Party. So British Communism had to build itself up
from scratch and has never enjoyed more than minimal support from the
working class – however attractive it may have been to intellectuals in the
1930s. The natural British distrust of general theories and inclination
towards the empiricism of 'hard facts' has meant that Marxism has had its
chief impact in Britain in the study of history, and to a lesser extent,
economics.

Most striking of all is Marxism's lack of success in the major capitalist
society, the United States. As long ago as 1906 the sociologist Werner Som-
bart wrote a book called *Why is there No Socialism in the United States?* His
own answer was that socialism had 'foundered upon shoals of roast beef and
apple pie'. In fact, at the time when socialism might have been expected to
take root in America – around the turn of the century – the average American worker was not particularly affluent. It is important to remember that,
unlike Europe, the United States has no feudal past. The American struggle
for democracy was not conducted against the background of entrenched

social privilege. Thus the very openness of the American political system had made it responsive to the demands of organised workers. In Europe, by contrast, the working class was more or less excluded from the political process and forced into a socialist solidarity in order to make any headway with its demands. The Americans, as de Tocqueville said, were 'born free', and since the United States was founded as a reaction to intolerance in Europe, this freedom was essentially a negative one, freedom *from* rather than freedom *for*, a doctrine of individualism rather than of Communism. The existence of the Frontier was also a factor which militated against socialism. The discontented worker could always imagine (and sometimes find) a better future 'out West'. Labour discontent was syphoned off and a ruggedly independent class of small farmers created. Finally, the United States is a land of immigrants. Ethnic divisions held up working–class unity and the successive waves of immigrants provided a kind of hierarchy, with the newest arrived, particularly from Southern and Eastern Europe, at the bottom and a labour aristocracy developing among the more established skilled workers. Even when immigration was drastically reduced after the First World War, the internal migration into the cities of unskilled labour from the land meant the injection into the industrial work force of the individualist, conservative attitudes bred in rural communities. By the time that organised labour emerged as a real force on the political scene, it could be assimilated into the reformist policies of Roosevelt's New Deal.

Although Marxism had not had much success as a political movement in the Western World, there has been considerable interest in Marxist theory over the last two decades. It is this theoretical bias that characterises what has come to be known as 'Western Marxism'. Finding it impossible to change the world, most Western Marxist thinkers have confined themselves to interpreting it. In the golden age of European Marxism during the three decades from the death of Engels in 1895 to the rise of Stalinism in the late 1920s, all the principal Marxist theorists (of whom Lenin was only the most prominent) were also leading members of Marxist political movements. They were thus forced constantly to test their theories against the reality of political involvement. The last fifty years in Western Europe, however, have seen a divorce between Marxist theory and political practice. The only mass Marxist movements were the Communist Parties whose rigid orthodoxy made them impossible bases for Marxists wishing to develop fresh ideas. The result was a wholesale migration of Marxism out of political parties and into the universities. Before the First World War, Marxists had had a profound contempt for 'professorial socialists'. After the Second World War, most of the leading Marxist thinkers were academics rather than politicians.

This shift of occupation coincided with a shift of interest in the subject matter of Marxism. Marx himself had begun his life as a student of Hegelian philosophy and then turned to the more practical matters of politics and economics. Many Western Marxists have trodden the opposite path and turned their backs on the unpromising fields of politics and economics. These were indeed unpromising areas for Marxist analysis in the 1950s and 1960s. These two decades saw an unprecedented consolidation of capitalist growth throughout the advanced industrial world which was disconcerting for Marxists who had inherited a tradition which stressed the moribund nature of the capitalist economy. The same two decades saw the establishment of stable formal democracy based on universal suffrage in all the advanced capitalist countries. Neither Marx nor Lenin had envisaged such a possibility and had consequently not provided the theoretical tools to deal with it. With the capitalist economies steadily prospering and the capitalist states politically secure and enjoying popular support, it is not surprising that most Marxist theorists took refuge in the more speculative realms of philosophy.

The classics of Marx such as the *Communist Manifesto* or *Capital* did not contain any philosophy as such. But the turn to a more philosophical interpretation of Marx was helped by the publication of some of Marx's early writings. These writings seemed to reveal a different sort of Marx – a philosopher and a humanist. They had some impact in Eastern Europe where Marxism, instead of being the creed of the underdog had been enthroned as the ruling ideology. There was obviously room to point out that Marx's picture of communist man did not seem to have much in common with state bureaucracies of the Stalinist type and the cautious thesis was put forward that alienation could exist even under socialism. This kind of Marxist humanism was particularly influential in Czechoslovakia during the Prague spring of 1968. Study of Marx's writings was seen as a return to the original source of Communist thought – much as the Reformers used the New Testament to show up abuses rife in the late mediaeval Church. In the West, these writings were eagerly seized upon by those disaffected with contemporary society. Marx's early works reflected his own criticisms of the dehumanising effects of early capitalism: they spoke just as strongly to those, particularly in the New Left, who perceived similar effects of later capitalism. The increasing power of technology and the possibility of manipulating man in society induced some commentators to take up what Marx said of the alienation of man in capitalist society and assimilate him into the general stream of opposition to the consumer society. Supposedly significant comparisons were even drawn between Marx and Zen Buddhism. The stultifying wealth and complexity of highly-developed societies made Marx's radical humanism more important for some than could have been anticipated in the nineteenth century.

Jean-Paul Sartre, the French existentialist philosopher whose later work tried to present a 'Marxism with a human face'

Hitherto, Marx and Marxism had been held to be opposed to all forms of 'bourgeois' thought. Now, however, with a fuller picture of Marx's work emerging, many Marxists attempted to assimilate non-Marxist approaches. There are two striking examples of this. The first is the work of the existentialist philosopher Jean-Paul Sartre. Existentialism was a plea for the freedom of the individual combining a protest at the tendency to treat human beings as things with a strong insistence on the reality of human responsibility. In his existentialist manifesto *Existentialism is a Humanism*, Sartre had written: 'Man simply is. Not that he is simply what he conceives himself to be, but he is what he wills, and as he conceives himself after already existing – as he wills to be after that leap towards existence. Man is nothing else but what he makes of himself.' This seems a long way from Marxism which emphasises the way in which human beings *en masse* are determined by their history and their social circumstances. Nevertheless, since Sartre came to consider Marxism to be 'the philosophy of our time', he tried to amalgamate it with his existentialist views. This involved 'reconquering man within Marxism' by restoring to Marxism the human dimension that had been present in the early Marx but squeezed out by later more dogmatic interpretations. The result was a massive work forbiddingly entitled *Critique of Dialectical Reason*. Tortuous and obscure, it is nevertheless full of the brilliant psychological insights and descriptions that always characterise Sartre's work. His main emphasis was still on the individual. As he said in a striking phrase, whereas for traditional Marxism the poet Valéry was no more than a petit bourgeois intellectual, existentialist Marxism would like to show why every petit bourgeois intellectual was not a Valéry. 'Contemporary Marxism', wrote Sartre, 'has entirely lost the meaning of what it is to be a man; to fill in the gaps it only has the absurd psychology of Pavlov'. With its lack of any serious historical dimension, its emphasis on freedom rather than determinism, and its insistence on starting with individuals, Sartre's work was a long way from classical Marxism. But it did crystallise a lot of rather vague attempts at the time to discover a 'Marxism with a human face'.

The work of Freud and his followers – our second example – might seem at first sight to be even more at odds with Marx. For Freud's view of the unconscious and infantile sexuality pointed to an explanation of human activity very different from Marx's economic determinism. For Freud, Marxism seemed yet another rationalisation that masked the fundamental springs of human action; and Marxists long dismissed Freudianism as an ideological product of *fin de siècle* Vienna. But one of Freud's disciples, Wilhelm Reich, was also a Marxist who emphasised the need to liberate the proletariat from repression in all spheres of life – particularly that of sex. He claimed that the only way to solve the oedipal problems discovered by Freud was the dissolution of the middle-class family. Reich placed his confidence in women and the young who, as more subjugated than the rest of society, had a better chance to see through the mechanics of repression. But Reich had no liking for Lenin. He thought Bolshevism prepared the way for Fascism by reinforcing authoritarianism in parties and trade unions. In a lecture tour of the Soviet Union in the late 1920s, Reich suggested that without a sexual revolution, Communism would degenerate into a bureaucratic state. This was enough to persuade the Soviet authorities to suppress psychoanalysis which had previously enjoyed some vogue in Russia. Reich, reviled by both orthodox Communists and orthodox psychoanalysts alike, was a lone voice. Erich Fromm, a prolific and popular writer, started life as both a Freudian and a Marxist, but by the time that he produced his most influential works, *Escape from Freedom*, for example, in 1941, he had moved beyond both. It was Marcuse who produced, in his *Eros and Civilization*, the most sustained attempt to unite Marx and Freud. Marcuse's study of the psychological obstacles to liberation led him to a utopian radicalism. Freud had seen sexual repression in society as eternally necessary due to the conflict between the pleasure principle and the reality principle. But for Marcuse, it was the social organisation of labour in capitalist society which subordinated instincts to reality. As technology advanced, this repression, justified under conditions of scarcity, became unnecessary and the way was open for a society which would be able to do away with repression by abolishing alienated labour. But this view, again, departs from Marx's original intent and any marriage of Marx and Freud has always resulted in the dominance of one at the expense of the other. After all, Freud did explicitly dismiss Marx with the pithy statement that 'aggression was not created by property'.

The attempt by Communist Parties to compromise with the political structures of capitalist societies has often led to the abandonment of their original objectives. Similarly, the efforts of Marxist intellectuals to combine their Marxism with non-Marxist philosophies has led to considerable adulteration of their original message. Western Marxist thinkers have often been pessimistic in outlook. This was natural given the political situation, but contrasts starkly with the optimism of classical Marxism. They have also been extraordinarily obscure, again in contrast to Marx who said that the accessibility of his writing to the working class was 'a consideration more important to me than any other'.

The particular characteristics of Western Marxism were largely due to the fact that history did not line up with Marxist expectations. However, in recent years the climate has changed somewhat as it has become clear that the recurring crisis of capitalism has not gone away. In the same year that Karl Marx died, another powerful thinker was born, the economist John Maynard Keynes. Keynes taught economic theory during the great world slump of the 1930s, when millions were thrown out of work in all the advanced capitalist countries, when it did appear to many people that perhaps at last Marx might be proved right, and when many of those people in Western countries were powerfully attracted to Marxist ideas. Keynes taught governments to spend their way out of the slump. That, and the Second World War, lifted the capitalist world out of the classic crisis. For a long time after, it was widely believed that modern capitalism was now so advanced that the old fashioned scourge of mass unemployment had gone for good. Modern capitalism had other problems to face, but it had solved the problems that Marx saw. Poverty and class conflict were things of the past.

It would be a brave man, or a very stupid one, who could say that now. In every advanced capitalist country there is large scale unemployment. In the West we have not got rid of classes either, and, more important, we have not succeeded in eliminating poverty. In the last ten years Marxists have begun to concentrate more on politics and economics but have yet to find the support among the working class that alone could give meaning to their ideas.

CONCLUSION

How are we to assess the importance of Marxism in the contemporary world? What message, if any, do Marx's ideas have for us a century after his death? Of course, the world has changed much since Marx wrote. Marx's age was the age of steam power and the electric telegraph. For him the great upheaval was caused when the traditional craftsmen of the sort he actually knew in the old Communist League were being replaced by unskilled or semi-skilled factory workers, the real modern industrial proletariat. A century after Marx died that industrial proletariat is being split up. In the West it is losing its identity. The microchip gives the blue collar workers white collars instead – and introduces chronic structural unemployment. The microchip takes them away from the factory, mill or mine. The means of production that Marx knew about, that Lenin knew about, are changing fast. By the end of this century the proportion of industrial workers will have declined considerably and the numbers of technical and professional workers will have increased. And this same technical progress has given the impersonal state in industrial societies vast and frightening powers of intervention and control. Marx shared the common nineteenth-century view that progress was somehow inexorably written into the story of human development. There would no doubt be setbacks and sufferings, but humanity, in its struggle to dominate nature, would in the long run produce a society in which human capacities were more extensively exercised and human needs more fully met. But more recent developments in the productive forces, and particularly atomic energy, have led many to wonder whether humanity's efforts to dominate nature have not taken a fundamentally wrong turning. We have lost our nerve and our own inventions have made us more dubious about 'progress' than at any time for the last two hundred years.

Many, too, of Marx's expectations have remained unfulfilled. Two cases are particularly striking. Firstly, there is the lack of revolutionary drive among the working-class in the West. Marx under-estimated the later role of Trade Unions and the possibilities of improvement in the position of the proletariat without recourse to revolution. The two class model he began with and the consequent idea of class struggle have proved simplistic with the persistence of the old middle classes and the emergence of new classes such as technicians and managers. With the lack of support for revolutionary politics among the mass of the working class, Marxist leaders have been faced with a dilemma: either they reflect the mood of the workers and produce reformist policies which dilute Marxism – or they preserve the revolutionary spirit of Marxism by setting themselves apart from, and superior to, the views of those they claim to represent. Secondly, Marx underestimated the persistence and growth of nationalism. Although sensitive to national sentiment in his own time, Marx considered that class divisions would prove stronger than national ones. August 1914 is a crucial date here: the fact that the world's largest Marxist party – in Germany – could be swept away on a nationalist tide led Marxists to revise their strategy. In all Marxist revolutions, there has been a strong nationalist element. Lenin himself was adept at co-opting the nationalism of the non-Russian peoples in the Tsarist empire. The revolutions in Yugoslavia, China, Cuba and Vietnam all had strong nationalist overtones.

With its emphasis on economic determinism and its confidence about the inevitability of socialism, Marxism has often indulged in a shallow optimism about the possibilities open to human nature. For Marxists have usually just assumed that there existed, as an alternative to capitalism, a morally superior and altogether more efficient method of organising production. Marx himself was a real child of the Enlightenment in this respect. After the pessimism of Nietzsche and Freud, the world is a great deal darker and the light of reason often reduced to a faint glimmer. For Marxism has been severely tarnished in practice – as, of course, has Christianity by the Crusades and the Inquisition, and liberal values by the activities of Western governments. Marxism remains, so far, much more impressive in its interpretations of the world than in its efforts to change it.

With its powerful synthesis of history, philosophy, sociology and economics, Marx's social theory was one of the most impressive intellectual achievements of the nineteenth century. When Sartre called Marxism 'the philosophy of our time', he had in mind the way in which many of the ideas of Marx have entered – albeit unconsciously – into the way in which, in the twentieth century, we look at the world. In a sense, we are all Marxists now. We tend to view man as a social being, not as an isolated individual; through the development of sociology, which owes so much to Marx, we study ways of changing and improving society; we appreciate historically the central role of economic factors in the development of humanity; we see the ways in which ideas are related to the interests of particular social and economic groups at particular times; and Marx's criticisms have taught many to see the inequalities and injustices in the capitalist system and at least to try to mitigate them.

For more than a century Marxism has been the language in which millions have expressed their hopes for a more just society. As a vehicle of protest, Marx's description of religion applies with equal force to the way in which many have seen his own message: 'the sigh of the oppressed creature, the feeling of a heartless world and the soul of soulless circumstances.' It is the reduction to scientific formulae and the institutionalisation of these aspirations that has caused the trouble. As Ignazio Silone, an old ex-Communist, put it: 'The more socialist theories claim to be "scientific", the more transitory they are; but socialist values are permanent. The distinction between theories and values is not sufficiently recognised, but is fundamental. On a group of theories, one can found a school; but on a group of values one can found a culture, a civilisation, a new way of living together.' It is well known that Marx himself was so angered by the uses to which his ideas were put by some of his would-be disciples that he exclaimed towards the end of his life: 'As for me, I am no Marxist!' But these same ideas – however distorted, revised or reinterpreted – continue to exercise their influence over men's hearts and minds. They have added a new dimension to the understanding of our world. Marx is the intellectual giant of both socialist theories and values. However doubtful some of the theories and however obscured some of the values, the history of Marxism over the last century is an integral and abiding part of humanity's search for this new way of living together.

CHRONOLOGICAL TABLE

1818 Birth of Marx
1842/3 Marx edits *Rheinische Zeitung*
1843 Marx moves to Paris
1845 Marx moves to Belgium
1846 Marx writes *The German Ideology*
1847 Marx joins Communist League
1848 Publication of *Communist Manifesto*
1848/9 Marx edits *Neue Rheinische Zeitung*
1849 Marx moves to London
1864 Foundation of First International
1867 Publication of Volume One of *Capital*
1870 Birth of Lenin
1871 Paris Commune
1883 Death of Marx
1889 Foundation of Second International
1893 Birth of Mao Tse-tung
1895 Death of Engels
1902 Bolshevik-Menshevik split
     Lenin writes *What is to be Done?*
1905 Revolution in Russia
1914 Outbreak of First World War
1915 Lenin writes *Imperialism*
1917 Lenin writes *State and Revolution*
     Bolsheviks come to power in Russia
1919 Abortive revolution in Germany
1921 Kronstadt revolt
     Beginning of NEP
1924 Death of Lenin
     Northern Expedition of Chiang Kai-shek
1926 Rise of Stalin to supreme power
1929 Trotsky expelled from Soviet Union
1930 Collectivisation of agriculture in Soviet Union
1935 Long March in China
1939 Outbreak of Second World War
1940 Murder of Trotsky
1942 Battle of Stalingrad
1948 Yugoslavia's break with Soviet Union

1949 People's Republic of China proclaimed
1953 Death of Stalin
1956 Condemnation of Stalin by Krushchev
     Soviet invasion of Hungary
1957 Launch of Soviet Sputnik
1958 Great Leap Forward in China
1959 Cuban revolution
1960 Sino-Soviet split
1962 Cuban missile crisis
1966 Cultural Revolution in China
1968 Soviet invasion of Czechoslovakia
     May events in Paris
1976 Death of Mao
1980 Death of Tito
1981 Martial law declared in Poland
1982 Death of Brezhnev

FURTHER READING

General
Two books covering the evolution of Marxist ideas are: Leszek Kolakowski, *Main Currents of Marxism*, Oxford University Press, 1978 and David McLellan, *Marxism After Marx*, Macmillan, 1980. A good overview of Communism since 1945 is provided by Adam Westoby, *Communism After World War Two*, Harvester, 1982. And there is a stimulating discussion of the broader issues in Robert Heilbroner, *Marxism: For and Against*, Norton, 1980.

Chapters One and Two
On Marx himself, the classic biography, by one of his disciples, is Franz Mehring, *Karl Marx: The Story of his Life*, 1934. It is a bit dated, but still worth reading. Two more recent biographies are David McLellan, *Karl Marx: His Life and Thought*, Macmillan, 1973 and Saul Padover, *Karl Marx. An Intimate Biography*, McGraw-Hill, 1978.

Chapter Three
The most vivid account of Russian Marxism up to 1914, dealing with Lenin, Trotsky and Stalin is Bertram Wolfe, *Three Who Made a Revolution*, Penguin, 1962. On Lenin, see Adam Ulam, *Lenin and the Bolsheviks*, Secker and Warburg, 1966 and Neil Harding, *Lenin's Political Thought*, two volumes, Macmillan, 1977 and 1980. For accounts of the 1917 revolution, see Trotsky's masterpiece *The History of the Russian Revolution*, Gollancz, 1965, and E. H. Carr, *The Bolshevik Revolution 1917–1923*, three volumes, Macmillan, 1950, 1952 and 1953. On Trotsky, see Isaac Deutscher's three volumes *The Prophet Armed*, *The Prophet Unarmed* and *The Prophet Outcast*, Oxford University Press, 1954, 1959 and 1963. Also the scholarly study of Baruch Knei-Paz, *The Social and Political Theory of Leon Trotsky*, Oxford University Press, 1978.

Chapter Four
The most accessible biography of Stalin is Isaac Deutscher, *Stalin*, Penguin, 1966. On how the Soviet Union is governed see Mary McAuley, *Politics and the Soviet Union*, Penguin, 1977. Two readable and well-informed books by American journalists are Robert Kaiser, *Russia: The People and the Power*, Secker and Warburg, 1976 and Hedrick Smith, *The Russians*, Quadrangle, 1976.

Chapter Five
On pre-1945 Chinese Communism, see the classic eye-witness account in Edgar Snow, *Red Star over China*, Penguin, 1972. Another classic is the description of the initial impact of communism on a single village in William Hinton, *Fanshen*, 1972. A good general book is the biography of Mao by Stuart Schram, *Mao Tse-tung*, Penguin, 1966. Two books by journalists on current Chinese politics and society are John Fraser, *The Chinese: Portrait of a People*, Fontana, 1982 and David Bonavia, *The Chinese*, Penguin, 1982.

On Cuba, see the background account of Robin Blackburn, *Slavery and Empire: The Making of Modern Cuba*, London, 1978. Two other reliable books are Maurice Zeitlin, *Revolutionary Politics and the Cuban Working Class*, Princeton University Press, 1970 and Edward Gonzalez, *Cuba under Castro*, Houghton Mifflin, 1974.

On Yugoslavia, there is the substantial study by Phyllis Auty, *Tito: A Biography*, Penguin, 1970. On the realities of self-management, see S. Zukin, *Beyond Marx and Tito*, Cambridge University Press, 1975.

Chapter Six
On the problems of Eurocommunism, see *Eurocommunism: Myth or Reality?*, ed. Paolo della Torre, Penguin, 1979. Two very different books on Western Marxist thinkers are the hostile Neil McInnes, *The Western Marxists*, Alcove Press, 1972 and the sympathetic Perry Anderson, *Considerations on Western Marxism*, New Left Books, 1976. A good short introduction to Marxism in America is John Diggins, *The American Left in the Twentieth Century*, Harcourt, Brace, 1973.

INDEX

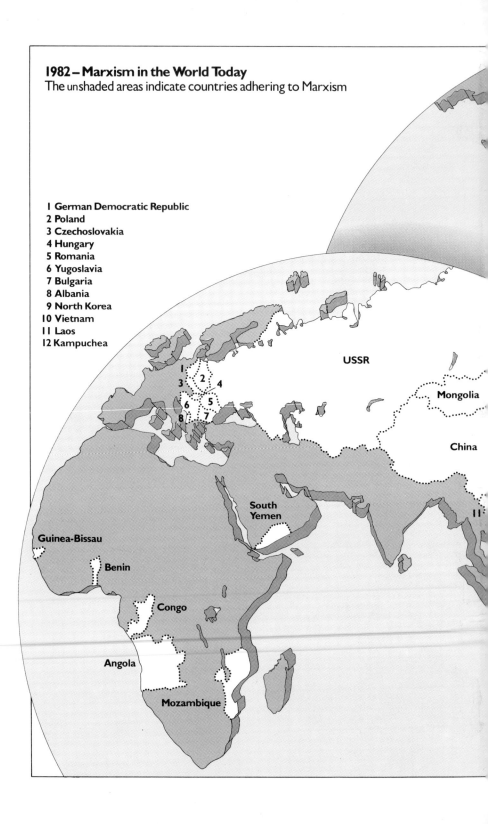

1982 – Marxism in the World Today
The unshaded areas indicate countries adhering to Marxism

1 German Democratic Republic
2 Poland
3 Czechoslovakia
4 Hungary
5 Romania
6 Yugoslavia
7 Bulgaria
8 Albania
9 North Korea
10 Vietnam
11 Laos
12 Kampuchea

USSR

Mongolia

China

South
Yemen

Guinea-Bissau

Benin

Congo

Angola

Mozambique

11